THE EMOTIONALLY SAVVY DIVORCE

SMART NEGOTIATIONS FOR A CLEAN BREAK

Praise for **The Emotionally Savvy Divorce**

"This book is a compassionate, practical guide to navigating divorce in a healthier way. Even in high-conflict situations, *The Emotionally Savvy Divorce* shows how you can negotiate strategically and move forward with clarity and confidence."

BILL EDDY, lawyer, therapist, mediator, co-founder of the High Conflict Institute, and author of *Splitting* and *BIFF for Coparent Communication*

"One of the most helpful divorce books I've read... I truly wish this book had existed during my own divorce."

JACKIE PILOSSOPH, founder of Divorced Girl Smiling

"Divorce can be reactive. Katherine E. Miller shows a different way. She offers a brighter and workable vision of divorce, ending in an agreement where both partners are seen and heard. Bravo."

MARK BANSCHICK, MD, author of *The Intelligent Divorce*

"Katherine E. Miller shows how to turn even the most charged feelings into clarity and wise decisions. You'll want this compassionate and empowering guide by your side."

JEFFREY DAVIS, strategist, speaker, author of *Tracking Wonder*

"Divorcing without emotional bankruptcy? Yes, it's possible. This book is your financial and emotional advisor in one—a must-read for anyone ready to turn the page with grace, grit, and dignity."

STACY FRANCIS, president and CEO of Francis Financial and founder of Savvy Ladies

"Engaging and beautifully written, *The Emotionally Savvy Divorce* is an essential blueprint for navigating divorce while preserving everyone's humanity. I only wish it had been available during my own divorce. A must-read."

JENNY DOUGLAS, founder of The Brooklyn Cottage

Katherine E. Miller, JD

THE
EMOTIONALLY
SAVVY
DIVORCE

PAGE TWO

Copyright © 2026 by Katherine E. Miller, JD

All rights reserved. No part of this book may be reproduced, stored in a retrieval system or transmitted, in any form or by any means, without the prior written consent of the publisher or a license from The Canadian Copyright Licensing Agency (Access Copyright). For a copyright license, visit accesscopyright.ca or call toll free to 1-800-893-5777.

Cataloguing in publication information is available from Library and Archives Canada.
ISBN 978-1-77458-605-1 (paperback)
ISBN 978-1-77458-606-8 (ebook)

Page Two
pagetwo.com

Page Two™ is a trademark owned by Page Two Strategies Inc., and is used under license by authorized licensees

Cover, interior design, and illustrations by Fiona Lee
Printed and bound in Canada by Friesens
Distributed in Canada by Raincoast Books
Distributed in the US and internationally by Macmillan

26 27 28 29 30 5 4 3 2 1

katherinemiller.com

Disclaimer

THIS BOOK is intended for informational and educational purposes only and does not constitute legal, financial, or therapeutic advice. Every divorce is unique, and readers are encouraged to seek guidance from qualified professionals for their specific situations.

The stories, case examples, and individuals described throughout this book are composites drawn from the author's experience working with a wide range of clients. These composite characters are designed to illustrate common themes, emotional patterns, and negotiation dynamics in divorce while protecting the privacy and confidentiality of all actual clients.

Out of deep respect for those who have entrusted the author with their most personal challenges, identifying details have been altered or blended, and any resemblance to real persons, living or deceased, is purely coincidental.

*For everyone navigating the difficult path of divorce.
May you find strength, clarity, and the courage
to build a future that truly aligns with who you are.*

*To the clients I have worked with throughout my
career—thank you for trusting me with your stories
and for teaching me so much about the journey
of divorce. Your resilience and insight have shaped my
understanding in ways I never could have imagined.*

THE
EMOTIONALLY
SAVVY
DIVORCE

Contents

Introduction
1

PART ONE DIVORCE IS EMOTIONAL

1. **It Doesn't Have to Be Messy**
   9
2. **Navigating Knots and Traps**
   33
3. **Charting Your Emotional Divorce Journey**
   55
4. **Anxiety Gets in the Way**
   71
5. **Lean Into Your Emotions**
   91

PART TWO NEGOTIATING WITH EMOTIONS

6. **Elevating the Conversation**
   109
7. **Understanding Interests in Divorce Negotiations**
   129
8. **Building Your Strategy: The Best and the Worst Alternatives**
   141

9	**The Proposal Blueprint**
	151
10	**Navigating Conflict in Negotiation**
	177
11	**The Final Stages: Is This the Right Deal?**
	199

Conclusion: The Journey Ahead

215

Acknowledgments

219

Appendix 1:
Choosing Your Divorce Process

221

Appendix 2:
Emotional Regulation Techniques

227

References and Further Reading

231

Introduction

Marcy took a seat across from me at my favorite restaurant in Midtown Manhattan. It had been about six months since I last saw her, during her visit to my office to sign her divorce papers. She looked more relaxed than I had ever seen her, and after settling in she looked up and smiled.

"How are you doing?" I asked her. "You look great!"

She laughed. "I have you to thank for that. But seriously, I'm much happier than I ever thought possible given everything that's happened over the last couple of years."

Marcy had come to me about two years earlier, having just discovered that her husband, Steve, a successful lawyer at a large firm in New York City, was having an affair with one of his associates. Unsure of what to do, she had confided in only two of her closest friends, who urged her to speak with a lawyer.

"When I first met you," Marcy continued, "I was so confused and hurt—angry but also ashamed. Part of me wanted to destroy Steve, to rent one of those billboards in Times Square and announce to the world how he'd wronged me." She paused, shaking her head and laughing a little to herself. "But honestly, the worst part was feeling so lost and worrying about our kids, Emma and Harrison."

Steve and Marcy met when he was a senior and she was a junior at Princeton. He attended NYU School of Law after graduating, and they continued dating. After her graduation, she worked in publishing in New York City while he finished law school, and they married a month after his graduation, just after he took the bar exam. They had two young children, Harrison and Emma. After the children were born, they moved to Scarsdale, New York, so their kids could attend the excellent public schools there. Steve became a corporate lawyer, while Marcy gave up her job in publishing during her pregnancy with Emma. She became a stay-at-home mom until she started a small party planning business to earn some income and keep herself occupied outside of her parental duties.

During our consultation, Marcy expressed extreme concern for Harrison and Emma. She was contemplating staying with Steve for their sake, but it had become nearly intolerable to live under the same roof since discovering his affair. She desperately wanted to find a way to stay a family without enduring the agony she was currently feeling. Although she had spent years in the role of a busy wife and mother, she wasn't sure her party business defined her as an independent adult woman outside of her family.

We discussed the different process options for handling the divorce—litigation, mediation, and collaborative divorce—and Marcy believed collaborative divorce was the best choice. Steve agreed, and over the next nine months, we negotiated an agreement that allowed them to navigate their separation and eventual divorce with respect and a mutual commitment to being the best parents they could be for Harrison and Emma. I admired Marcy for the work she had done on herself and the discipline she showed in processing her hurt and anger. Initially motivated by her children, she ultimately realized she was also healing for herself.

"Katherine, I have a neighbor going through the worst divorce right now," Marcy told me. "They've been at it for two years, arguing over custody, money, and even the furniture in the house—everything you can think of." She sighed. "The kids have a lawyer, and there's a forensic evaluator for custody issues and a forensic accountant for the finances. What a nightmare! I'm so glad that Steve and I could maintain our dignity and mutual respect throughout our divorce. It wasn't easy at times, that's for sure, but it was worth it."

Why was Marcy's experience of divorce so different from her neighbor's and that of so many others we know? There are many variables, but a significant factor was Marcy's willingness to confront her emotions and work through them to identify her core values and what was truly important to her. She also looked at her role in the estrangement from Steve and took responsibility for it. Although he had the affair, she was able to recognize her contribution to the deterioration of their relationship. Ultimately, Marcy moved beyond blame—beyond a framework where one person is right and the other wrong—to a place of acceptance. And she was able to use that skill to be a heck of a negotiator!

I am on a mission to change the perception of divorce. Over three decades of working with clients through divorce negotiation and mediation, I've witnessed the ugliness that can arise from the process. Stigmas need to be eliminated, and the way we view divorce must be reframed. My goal is to transform the culture of divorce and how people manage the crucial negotiations surrounding it.

Negotiation is a part of everyday life. We negotiate with salespeople, our kids, our partners, our bosses, our parents (maybe even sometimes ourselves)—often without even realizing it. We've all developed negotiation skills of some form. Yet, when it comes to divorce, those skills tend to disappear. The familiar rules—where logic, compromise, and mutual benefit lead to resolution—no longer seem to apply. Emotions run high, the past feels as important as the future, and even a "fair" deal can feel like a loss. To successfully navigate the end of a marriage, we have to approach negotiation differently.

Yes, the process of negotiating divorce terms is often longer and more challenging than many other negotiations in life. There is so much at stake, including our identities, and the negotiation (and conflict) cannot be ignored. We cannot simply walk away from the table as we might in other forms of negotiation. If a job doesn't work out, we can apply elsewhere. If a house purchase falls through, we can find another property. If a car salesman is rude, we can choose to go to a competitor. But in divorce, the only available option to us is negotiation with our spouse.

There is also more on the line in a divorce than in a job or even a major purchase. When two people have built a life together, they share money, property, investments, and possibly debt accumulated over years, perhaps decades. They may share children and the shattered dream of their family. All of this representing considerable emotional involvement. So, while conventional wisdom tells us to eliminate feelings from the equation, to "leave your emotions out of it" when negotiating, here lies the problem: this is simply not feasible in a divorce.

After three decades of helping clients navigate divorce, my advice goes against conventional wisdom: Your emotions are valuable. Lean into those emotions. Work through them; let them guide you in determining what you truly want in the end. I understand that navigating these emotions can be treacherous, and I don't advocate allowing oneself to be overwhelmed by the riptides of anger and anxiety. But acknowledging your feelings—rather than suppressing them—and listening to what they are telling you, is essential to successful resolution. Your feelings hold insight into what you need and what will make sense for you moving forward.

In this book, I will share how and why to lean into these emotions throughout your divorce negotiation process, using "people terms" rather than legal jargon. Why? Because you can achieve the outcome you desire without engaging in a hard-fought battle in the courtroom that drags your partner and family through the mud. You can take the high road and reach the best outcome.

Nobody enters marriage expecting to get divorced, yet 50 percent of marriages end this way. For those who don't know what to expect, fear and anxiety can compound already unfortunate circumstances. In *The Emotionally Savvy Divorce* I will uncover the truths about divorce negotiation and offer you both comfort and education throughout the process. I will guide you through negotiations to get what you want while maintaining healthy relationships with those you care about. What will you gain from this book? A new way of looking at divorce—one that shifts the process from a battle to a negotiation that benefits both parties. Because so many people come out the other side of divorce wondering if they received a good deal or a bad one, this is also a topic I will address in the final chapter. When the process works better, the outcome does too.

A Note About Language: Referring to Your Ex

Throughout this book, you'll see that I often refer to your spouse as "the ex," even if your divorce isn't final yet. Technically, yes, you're still legally married. But emotionally—and often practically—the shift is already well underway. Referring to them as the "ex" reflects that emotional reality, much like calling someone an ex-boyfriend or ex-girlfriend when the relationship ends, even if no paperwork is involved. To keep things clear and grounded in the emotional experience of divorce, I'll use the ex, or your ex, throughout. I hope this language helps center you in your own process—and keeps the focus on moving forward.

PART ONE

DIVORCE
IS
EMOTIONAL

1

It Doesn't Have to Be Messy

Every divorce negotiation is unique, not only because of the facts involved but also because of the people at the table. Each person brings their own history, motivations, and conflict patterns into the process. Although there are common themes that divorce lawyers see repeatedly, it is a common mistake to assume that a recognizable pattern leads to a predictable outcome. The best among us know that individual experiences and desires of those involved create a unique dynamic that must be understood in order to achieve a successful resolution. You have the power to change your negotiation and influence the results. Even if your ex is the most unreasonable person on the face of the earth, you can steer the negotiations in your favor. One thing that will help you do that is to know yourself and to take proactive steps to set yourself up for success.

Know the People

In family and divorce negotiations, where the emotional stakes are high, it's crucial to understand the people involved—not just their legal or financial positions, but what it is beneath the surface that drives them. Whether you're a party to the divorce or a professional guiding the process, insight into each person's motivation, including your own, can lead to more productive negotiations and better outcomes.

Consider Owen and Alice's situation. Owen comes from a family where divorce had devastating financial consequences. Growing up, he and his siblings had to contribute financially to the household from an early age, which left a lasting impression on him. Now, as an adult, Owen has been married to Alice for eighteen years, and they have three teenage children. Throughout their marriage, Owen has been the primary breadwinner and financial manager, carefully building a nest egg for their future. However, the prospect of dividing this nest egg in the divorce terrifies him, and he is very protective of it. Despite his fear, Owen genuinely wants to treat Alice with love and respect during the divorce, aiming to be both generous and caring.

Alice, on the other hand, has a different perspective. Her parents' divorce was amicable, setting an example of how a good divorce could look. However, throughout her marriage to Owen, Alice has felt overshadowed, often believing that she was under his thumb. She seeks separation not out of anger but as a means to explore her own identity and take responsibility for herself—something she feels she has neglected while married. While Alice also desires a respectful and amicable divorce, she is determined to assert herself as Owen's equal in this process, even though their circumstances are quite different.

Then there's Susan and Evan, who have been together for fifty years. Their relationship has been a mix of challenges and successes, with Evan having retired from a prestigious position. They have one adult daughter who is married and has children of her own. Susan, who comes from a difficult family background, is highly sensitive to criticism and can easily feel attacked, which often hampers her ability to engage empathetically. She is acutely aware of others' perceptions of her but struggles to offer empathy in return.

Evan, despite his professional success, often feels like an underdog trying to prove himself to the world. He is wary of being taken advantage of, and when he feels unappreciated, he can become petty.

Their negotiation isn't just about dividing assets—it's about managing the deep-seated emotions and long-standing dynamics that have shaped their relationship.

In both couples' cases, while the financial security of the parties involved is not in question, the emotional landscape makes the negotiations anything but straightforward. It's not just the facts or finances that complicate divorce negotiations—it's the feelings, the pasts, and the personal values that each person brings to the table. Understanding these emotional drivers is essential in moving toward a fair and equitable resolution—something we are hardwired for.

Hardwired for Fairness

It turns out that human beings are predisposed to fairness. In *Science-Daily*, the Association for Psychological Science reports that "the brain finds self-serving behavior emotionally unpleasant, but a different bundle of neurons also finds genuine fairness uplifting. What's more, these emotional firings occur in brain structures that are fast and automatic, so it appears that the emotional brain is overruling the more deliberate, rational mind. Faced with a conflict, the brain's default position is to demand a fair deal."

In this context, it seems that being hardwired for fairness should make negotiations easier, but it also turns out that our view of "fair" is tipped toward our own self-interest. So while we desperately want a "fair" agreement, we strongly disagree on what is truly fair. A friend of mine puts it this way: "Fairness is in the mind of the beholder—but we agree on what is beautiful much more easily than we agree on what is fair." And because we only want what is fair and cannot agree on what that means, we feel the other person is treating us unfairly, leading to feelings of anger and hurt. This is part of the human condition and is also a place where examining our feelings might yield results that can help us get unstuck.

When I interviewed Chris Voss, the retired FBI hostage negotiator and author of *Never Split the Difference: Negotiating as if Your Life Depended On It*, he told me, "We don't have the ability to actually assess fairness on our own, and we'll never be satisfied with fairness." That is quite a contradiction that we must all grapple with. Since we are hardwired for fairness but cannot recognize or accept it when it's presented to us, what can we do?

Here is a simple exercise that might help if you are facing a conflict where you want a fair result and the other party seems to want a fair result too, but you just cannot agree on what fair is.

1. Ask yourself what values you hold that lead you to conclude that your position is fair. Are you protecting your sense of security? Autonomy? Responsibility? Fairness itself? What are you protecting and why?

2. Now, think about what you know about the other person. Even if you are angry with them, try to view them as a person who is also protecting their own values and has their own worries.

3. Now write down at least five values they might hold that they would want to protect. Write down the values as you believe the other person would articulate them, and not from your perspective. If you cannot imagine what their values are, then write down what values you would be protecting if you were doing and saying what they are doing and saying.

Your values are a fundamental part of who you are, shaping how you see yourself and the world. When you feel attacked, it's natural to respond with anger or fear, but often the underlying value at stake isn't immediately clear. Taking the time to reflect on what's happening can provide deeper insight into your own needs and, potentially, a better understanding of the other person's perspective. Those insights will prove highly beneficial as you work through your divorce negotiations.

The Evolution of Divorce Negotiations

When people first decide to divorce, they are often, if not always, in a heightened emotional state. Whether they feel liberated or devastated, the emotional intensity inevitably leads to anxiety. While it's natural to want a quick resolution, it's important to understand that time can be an ally in helping you reach a sound agreement. And, as difficult as the process may be, allowing the negotiations to unfold over time and proceed at a reasonable pace gives the parties involved the emotional space needed to make thoughtful decisions rather than reactive ones.

Contrary to popular belief, the fastest divorce is not necessarily the best. Rushing through the process can result in hasty decisions that don't hold up over time. There is a road map to the divorce negotiation process, and while it might be tempting to take shortcuts, doing so comes with risks. What follows is a basic structure of the process.

Each step in this process can involve a lot of detail, and at times it may feel like you're lost in a forest of issues, but this basic structure serves as a guide. Knowing where you are in the process, and what needs to happen next, can help you stay focused on your ultimate goal.

When you are navigating the difficult discussions ahead, it's crucial to establish an infrastructure for resolving conflict with your ex. Most divorcing couples cannot make the necessary decisions on their own—they need help identifying the issues that must be resolved and negotiating those decisions. Choosing the right process helps you manage expectations, work toward resolution, and maintain a greater sense of calm. When setting up this process, you will need to

- establish how you will communicate (or leave all negotiations to the professionals);

- agree on the information needed to make informed decisions;

- learn to understand each other's perspectives, not just on the issues but on how the problems are framed.

ROAD MAP TO DIVORCE NEGOTIATION

Choose a process → Gather information (outside and inside)* → Negotiate → Resolve → Draft → Finalize and sign → Live it

---

* outside being bank accounts, value of the house (and how much is on the mortgage), and how much it costs to maintain the current standard of living; *inside* is what is important to each person and why—their values and priorities

You'll also need to consider the *how*, *why*, and *what* of any discussion that you undertake.

- **How:** the structure of the discussion and the dynamic between the participants.
- **Why:** the deeper purpose behind the discussion as well as the dynamic between you and each of your motivations.
- **What:** the subject matter of the discussion.

In any negotiation, it's important to distinguish between what needs to be decided (and why), when it should be addressed, and how the process will unfold. For example, earlier, I mentioned Marcy and Steve's choice to work within the collaborative divorce process, a choice that gave them the flexibility to find their own solutions on their own timeline with professional support. While collaborative divorce is not right for everyone, establishing the *how* at the beginning of this particular process is critical. When I begin working with a couple in conflict, or even just one client, I take time to clarify how we're going to work together. This strategic step sets the stage for a smoother, more efficient process.

Starting with the *what* rarely works because it often leads parties to dive back into their familiar arguments. If they could resolve things on their own, they likely would have done so already. Most people enter the divorce process with a heightened sense of defensiveness and a natural resistance to more pain. To achieve the best outcome, it's vital that the process calms the parties rather than inflames them.

There will be challenging moments, particularly when negotiating contentious issues, and it's common for people to feel stuck or that the process is failing. Divorce can bring a lot of anxiety. These feelings are understandable; however, with an established process for handling difficult conversations, the anxiety can be reduced, and it becomes easier to get back on track toward resolution.

As people move through the phases of divorce negotiations, their relationship to the process and their priorities will likely evolve. The process itself can change them, helping them gain clarity on what is truly important and what no longer seems so crucial. For instance, in the early stages of deciding to divorce, anxiety often drives people to focus on specific outcomes that they believe will make them feel secure. A fear of losing their lifestyle might lead someone to insist on staying in the house at all costs. And a fear of losing status might result in demands for lifetime alimony.

It's essential to examine these fears, understand what's underneath them, and identify the hopes and desires that lie on the other side. Mark and Cheryl, for example, came to me after two years of

---

While it's natural to want a quick resolution, it's important to understand that time can be an ally in helping you reach a sound agreement.

litigation, having spent a small fortune on legal fees. Initially driven by anger and hurt, they were now ready to move on. Through a few sessions, we negotiated a deal that worked for both of them, even if it wasn't perfect for either. Had they come to mediation earlier, the process might have taken longer.

It takes time to see clearly what truly matters and to crystallize your priorities. Like Michelangelo finding David in a block of marble, you need to look for the precious needs and wants in the fear and anxiety. They are there, waiting to be discovered and defined. And along with that process comes a need to confront conflict.

Choosing the Right Process

One of the most critical decisions you will make in your divorce is choosing the right process, as it can significantly impact the outcome, cost, and emotional toll of the proceedings. The divorce process you select—whether it's litigation, mediation, collaborative divorce, or negotiation—will shape how you and your ex navigate the dissolution of your marriage and resolve key issues like child custody, asset division, and support.

If you are at the point where you are just thinking through what divorce process is best for you, you'll find a questionnaire in the back of the book (appendix 1) that helps you do that. But first, here is a brief rundown of your options:

- **Litigation** is often viewed as the traditional route, involving court battles and legal representation, which can be adversarial and expensive but may be necessary in cases with significant conflict or power imbalances, or sometimes if one spouse is not ready to address issues around mental health or substance abuse.

- **Mediation** offers a more collaborative approach, allowing couples to work with a neutral third-party mediator to reach mutually acceptable agreements. This process can be less costly and time-consuming, fostering open communication and cooperation.

- **Collaborative divorce** involves both parties and their attorneys working together to negotiate a settlement without going to court, prioritizing respectful dialogue and shared solutions.

- **Negotiation** allows the parties to engage directly or through attorneys to settle divorce issues, offering flexibility and control over the process.

The process you choose will also shape your future interactions with your spouse, whether at a sporting event, a graduation, or the birth of your first grandchild. And as you consider what process to choose, let me share one of the surprising truths I've learned through years of mediating: the transformative power of neutrality. When people are locked in conflict—especially in divorce negotiations—it can seem impossible to agree on anything without feeling like you're conceding too much. That's where mediation becomes invaluable. A skilled neutral mediator can often break the deadlock by creating a space where both parties feel heard and respected. This neutral perspective doesn't mean ignoring emotions or compromising on values—it simply allows both parties to step back, see the bigger picture, and move toward resolution. Mediation works not just because it addresses the issues at hand but because it transforms the emotional dynamics between the parties, helping them shift from entrenched conflict to constructive dialogue. I'll talk more about mediation in chapter 10.

Whatever process you choose, make sure you understand the ground rules of that process and that everyone agrees what they are. Understanding the ground rules of your chosen divorce process is essential to ensuring a smooth and effective resolution. Ground rules establish the framework for how discussions and negotiations will be conducted, outlining expectations for communication, confidentiality, decision-making, and behavior.

Making sure that everyone is on the same page regarding these rules is crucial because it fosters a collaborative environment and reduces misunderstandings and conflicts. When both parties understand and agree to the rules, it creates a sense of security and predictability, allowing for more focused and productive discussions.

Here are some examples of ground rules:

- **Communication protocols:** With these rules you will agree on how and when to communicate, such as through email or scheduled meetings, and establish rules for respectful language and active listening. For example, both parties might agree to speak one at a time and avoid interrupting each other during discussions.

- **Confidentiality agreements:** Ensure that all information shared during negotiations remains confidential. This can help both parties feel secure in openly discussing sensitive issues without fear of exposure.

- **Decision-making processes:** Determine how decisions will be made and documented. For instance, both parties might agree that all decisions must be documented in writing and signed by both parties before implementation.

- **Behavioral expectations:** Set expectations for professional and respectful behavior. For example, parties might agree to avoid personal attacks and focus on issues rather than emotions during negotiations.

- **Meeting etiquette:** Establish rules for meeting conduct, such as starting and ending on time, preparing materials in advance, and maintaining a constructive focus on resolving issues.

Clear ground rules help manage expectations and establish boundaries, promoting respectful interactions and minimizing emotional escalation. They also serve as a reference point to address any deviations or disputes that may arise during the process, helping to keep the proceedings on track. Ultimately, when everyone adheres to agreed-upon ground rules, it builds trust and facilitates a more efficient and amicable resolution, paving the way for successful outcomes that align with all parties' interests and needs.

It is important to establish ground rules even when everyone appears to be on the same page because people are different. Take Teresa and Sebastian for example. Teresa is an intensely private person. She hasn't told anyone about the divorce except her minister and her sister. She is journaling extensively and working out in her mind how she is going to frame the message so she can create a boundary that protects her from being overwhelmed by other people's concern or judgment. Sebastian, however, processes his feelings by talking about them, and, as a result, he's told more people than he can remember what is going on between him and Teresa.

One Wednesday afternoon, Teresa goes to get her dry cleaning. She has an important meeting at work the next day and wants to wear her best suit. She's thinking about that meeting as she walks into her local dry cleaner's, ticket in hand, ready to pay and leave, when the dry cleaner comes out from around the counter and hugs her. Cindy has worked the counter there for years, and she and Teresa have always exchanged pleasantries during the laundry drop-off. That morning Cindy says, "Sebastian was here earlier and he told me what's going on with you two. I am so sorry to hear you are getting divorced. You really should go to mediation—it is so much better for the kids. Have you told them yet?"

It's lovely that Cindy cares so much; but whether her advice is good or bad, it doesn't matter because Teresa is just shocked that Cindy knows what's going on and is offering her concern (and unsolicited advice) before Teresa herself has even crafted a way to manage her feelings about the news being public. Teresa is now also faced with the possibility that the kids will hear about the divorce from someone else (if they have not already been told), and this throws her into a panic. Imagine the scene at home that evening when Teresa confronts Sebastian about his loose lips.

And once attorneys are involved in the dispute? Unnecessary bad feelings, legal fees, and delays could be the result, all of which could have been avoided with a simple agreement about who Sebastian and Teresa will use to help them figure their situation out. Now, I'm not suggesting that either Sebastian or Teresa is wrong about how they are handling the situation. People work through challenging issues in different ways. However, if they had discussed who each of them was going to talk to (or not), they would have avoided this problem.

Working with Your Lawyer Effectively

Speaking of attorneys, they can be intimidating. Here are some things to remember about the attorney-client relationship. Your lawyer is your partner in navigating the legal complexities of divorce, but like any partnership, it works best when you stay actively engaged and aligned on what truly matters. Lawyers bring invaluable expertise, but they're also human, which means they may sometimes need a little guidance to stay focused on your priorities. At the end of the day, you know your life better than anyone else, and your goals—not theirs—should lead the way.

One thing I tell my clients is this: Your lawyer works for you. They're there to advocate for you, guide you through the process, and make sure your interests are protected. But the final decisions? Those are yours to make. And that can feel overwhelming—especially when you're emotionally exhausted and just want someone to tell you what to do.

But here's the truth: No matter how strong your lawyer's opinion may be, they aren't living your life. They won't be the one co-parenting with your ex or managing your financial future. That will be you.

Take Marcy, for example. Her lawyer initially pushed hard for her to keep the house, thinking it was a "win." But Marcy's perspective had shifted—she realized staying in the house no longer aligned with her long-term goals. By communicating this to her lawyer, she redirected the focus to negotiating financial security and stability for her kids. That clarity made all the difference.

Sometimes, the most powerful thing you can do in a legal negotiation is pause and ask yourself, What really matters to me here? Your lawyer can help you get to the answer, but it ultimately has to come from you.

Unsurprisingly, lawyers have egos, and sometimes those egos can get in the way. Maybe they're caught up in "winning" against the other side or proving something to the opposing counsel. Though their passion might come from a good place, ego can sometimes push things off track. If you notice your lawyer escalating conflicts or focusing too much on scoring points, take a step back and gently but firmly remind them of your priorities. Saying something as simple as "I'm not looking to win this fight—I just want a solution that works for me and my family" can help realign the conversation.

Here are some things to keep in mind when you are working with your lawyer.

Ask Questions and Stay Curious

It's okay to not understand every legal strategy or term your lawyer throws out. In fact, it's better to ask questions than to just nod along and hope for the best. Your lawyer is there to help you, but they can't read your mind. Asking questions ensures you're on the same page and making informed decisions. Here are some helpful questions to keep in your back pocket:

- How does this approach help me achieve my goals?
- Are there other ways we could handle this issue?
- What are the risks if we go down this path?

When you stay curious, you're not just a bystander in the process—you're an active participant in shaping your future.

Speak Up If Something Feels Off

If your lawyer is pushing for something that doesn't sit right with you, trust your instincts. Maybe they're being overly aggressive, or maybe they're focused on winning a legal argument while ignoring the emotional impact it might have on you or your family. It's okay to say, "This doesn't feel like the right approach for me." Your lawyer is there to support you, not to take over.

Marcy wanted to maintain a cooperative relationship with Steve for the sake of their kids. If her lawyer had suggested a more combative approach, Marcy could have said, "I appreciate your advice, but it's important to me that we don't burn bridges in this process. Let's find another way."

Sometimes, the most powerful thing you can do in a legal negotiation is pause and ask yourself, What really matters to me here?

It's Okay to Get a Second Opinion

Sometimes, despite your best efforts, you might feel like your lawyer just isn't the right fit. That doesn't mean you've failed or that they're a bad lawyer—it just means you might need someone who better understands your goals. Seeking a second opinion can give you fresh perspective and peace of mind.

I've had clients come to me mid-process, feeling like their lawyer wasn't truly hearing them. One client, for example, was stuck in a prolonged battle over spousal support because her lawyer was focused on "winning" the negotiation, even though it was prolonging the conflict and draining her emotional energy. Once we shifted the focus to finding a resolution that aligned with her values, the process finally started to move forward.

Remember, It's a Team Effort

At its best, your relationship with your lawyer should feel like a partnership. You bring the vision for your future, and they bring the legal tools to help you get there. By staying engaged, asking questions, and speaking up when something doesn't feel right, you can make sure that your lawyer's efforts are aligned with what truly matters to you.

NOW THAT you understand what the different divorce processes are and the importance of establishing ground rules (not to mention how to work with your lawyer), let's consider another critical aspect of the divorce process: sharing information. Understanding the role of information sharing, or discovery as it's known in the legal world, can help you avoid unnecessary delays and complications while ensuring that both parties have a clear view of the financial and personal landscape.

Regardless of which path you choose—litigation, mediation, negotiation, or collaborative divorce—the process is essentially the same: gather and exchange information, explore options, and negotiate an outcome. The first step—gathering and exchanging information—is critical. Your decisions about parenting, dividing assets, and financial support all depend on having accurate and complete information. In litigation, this stage is formally called *discovery*, but the underlying goal is the same across all approaches: to create transparency, ensure fairness, and lay the groundwork for informed decision-making throughout your divorce.

Let's explore why discovery is so vital to achieving a fair and equitable resolution.

What Is Discovery?

Divorce is full of critical decisions—who gets what, how finances will be handled, and what life after separation will look like. But before you can make those decisions, you need all the facts. That's where discovery comes in. Discovery is the process of gathering and exchanging essential information about finances, property, and other key issues. Whether done formally through legal procedures or informally through voluntary sharing, discovery ensures transparency and lays the foundation for a fair and informed divorce negotiation.

Discovery is the legal process that ensures transparency by requiring both spouses to disclose all relevant financial details, including assets, debts, and income. In litigation, this may involve formal steps—such as interrogatories (written questions under oath), document requests, and depositions—or it can be handled informally when both spouses cooperate and share information freely. In a cooperative divorce, discovery can be as simple as exchanging financial documents voluntarily. But when trust is low—or assets are complex—formal discovery provides legal mechanisms to ensure full disclosure. Regardless of the method, the goal remains the same: to give both parties, and their advisors or their lawyers, a full and accurate understanding of their marital finances and any other critical issues.

While the discovery process is essential for transparency, its timeline can vary widely depending on factors like cooperation, complexity of the case or finances, and the legal requirements of the state or local court system. In some instances, if there are significant assets or disputes—over business ownership, investments, or hidden assets—discovery may take longer as it requires more detailed analysis and documentation. On the other hand, in cases where both parties are cooperative and have straightforward financial situations, the discovery process can move more quickly. Understanding these variables and their potential effects helps set realistic expectations as you move through the divorce process.

The discovery process is crucial because it levels the playing field. It prevents one spouse from hiding assets, understating income, or otherwise withholding important information that could unfairly influence the outcome of the divorce.

Here's why thorough discovery is essential.

Ensuring Fair Division of Property

Before any decisions can be made about how to divide marital property, it's necessary to know exactly what property exists. This includes not just obvious assets like the family home or cars, but also bank accounts, retirement accounts, investments, business interests, cryptocurrency, non-traditional assets, and debts. Discovery ensures that all these assets and liabilities are disclosed and considered when crafting a settlement or preparing for trial. Imagine discovering late in the process that your spouse has a significant amount of stock options or a pension that you were unaware of. Without discovery, such assets might never come to light, leading to an inequitable division of property.

Accurate Calculation of Support

Child support and spousal support (alimony) are typically based on the income and financial needs of both parties. Accurate information about each spouse's income, expenses, and financial resources is critical to determining appropriate support amounts. Suppose one spouse owns a business and claims a lower income than they actually receive either by lying or by paying for many personal expenses through the business. Through discovery, the other spouse can request financial statements, tax returns, and other documents to accurately assess the business's true profitability and ensure that support calculations reflect the full financial picture.

Informed Decision-Making

Informed decision-making is at the heart of a fair and effective divorce settlement. Whether you're deciding how to divide time with your children, how to allocate assets, or how much support is needed, having complete and accurate information is essential to making decisions that will stand the test of time. If you're negotiating a parenting plan, knowing each parent's work schedule, travel commitments, and future plans can help you create a schedule that works for both parents and children. Without this information, you might agree to a plan that becomes unworkable in the future, leading to further conflict.

The Role of Cooperation in Discovery

Although discovery can be a formal legal process, it doesn't have to be contentious. In fact, many divorces benefit from a cooperative approach to information sharing, where both parties voluntarily share necessary information. This can make the process quicker, less expensive, and less stressful.

Cooperation during discovery can also foster goodwill between the parties, setting a tone of respect and collaboration. When both spouses work together to provide full transparency, it often leads to smoother negotiations in other areas, such as parenting plans, child support, and spousal support. By building a foundation of trust and openness during discovery, both parties are more likely to find mutually acceptable solutions, reducing the emotional strain and potential conflict as they move forward.

However, if one spouse is unwilling to cooperate, the other can request court-ordered discovery during litigation to ensure that all relevant information is disclosed. This may involve subpoenas for documents or depositions, where individuals are required to answer questions under oath. It's important to approach discovery with diligence and honesty. Failing to disclose assets or income can lead to severe legal consequences, including penalties or an unfavorable ruling. Courts take transparency seriously, and if one spouse is found to be hiding assets or being uncooperative, the judge can impose financial penalties, adjust the division of property, or even alter support arrangements. In extreme cases, hiding information can lead to accusations of fraud, which can further complicate the legal proceedings and damage a person's credibility in court.

Dragging out the discovery process by being uncooperative can also increase legal costs, prolong the divorce, and strain negotiations, making it harder to reach an amicable resolution. Long-term, this can affect the overall settlement, as courts are more likely to favor the spouse who has acted in good faith. Being upfront from the beginning ensures that the process remains fair and efficient, reducing the emotional and financial toll on both parties.

Tips for Successful Discovery

Information sharing and discovery are the backbone of any successful divorce process. By ensuring that both parties have access to all relevant information, discovery enables informed decision-making, fair division of property, and accurate support calculations. Whether you're engaging in formal discovery through the legal system or cooperating informally, approaching this phase with transparency and diligence is key to achieving a fair and equitable divorce settlement. Here are some key things to remember as you work through the discovery process:

- **Be thorough:** Gather all necessary documents early in the process, including bank statements, tax returns, pay stubs, mortgage documents, and any other financial records.

- **Be honest:** Disclose all assets and debts, even those you might be tempted to hide. Full transparency is not only legally required but also essential for a fair outcome.

- **Stay involved and ask questions:** Though your attorney will often handle most of the discovery process, it's crucial that you stay engaged and informed. Don't hesitate to ask questions or seek clarification about what is being requested or disclosed. You will also be responsible for sharing information requested by your ex's attorney.

- **Stay organized:** Keep track of all documents and communications related to discovery. This will help you stay on top of the process and ensure that nothing is overlooked.

When you are participating actively in the process of discovery, you help your attorney build a stronger case on your behalf. Remember, discovery is a collaborative effort, and your involvement is key to making sure all the relevant information is brought to light.

Now that you've laid the groundwork through discovery, it's time to turn inward and identify what truly matters to you—shifting from the practical task of gathering information to the more personal question of what you want your future to look like.

What Do You Want?

Stephen R. Covey's work been a cornerstone in business negotiation strategies since the publication in 1989 of his landmark *7 Habits of Highly Effective People*. One of Covey's key pieces of advice is to begin with the end in mind—to focus on what you want for your life rather than what you want from others. Shifting your focus from what you want *from your spouse* to what you want *for yourself* can be one of the hardest but most transformative parts of divorce. This approach is best illustrated by Nancy and James's situation—where the emotional complexity of unmet expectations clashed with the desire to find a healthier path forward.

Nancy and James dated for two years before they moved in together. James came from a large and close-knit family. Nancy, an only child whose father died when she was ten, was drawn to James's big family and loved feeling included in the family gatherings. However, Nancy always thought that as their relationship developed James would turn some of that commitment toward her and the family she imagined they would create together. After Nancy and

James married and had a son, Max, she was sure that James would focus on their nuclear family. But much to Nancy's disappointment that never happened and James insisted that they continue to participate not only in all of his parents' gatherings but also those of his larger extended family.

As time passed, Nancy became frustrated and started to complain about these mandatory family get-togethers. Tension began to build in the marriage. The couple entered therapy, but James felt that he had never hidden how important his family was to him; this was "part of the deal" when she married him. Ultimately, the couple decided to divorce.

Now Nancy faced some difficult decisions about where and when Max would be with James for these family gatherings post-divorce. Max was used to celebrating every holiday with his father's family and his many cousins. Nancy had also enjoyed good relationships with James's siblings and cousins, although her resentment of the family demands had tainted them. In their marriage, Nancy had wanted a close emotional relationship with a partner who cherished their connection, but she also loved feeling part of a committed family. However, she was furious with James for being unwilling to prioritize his time with her and Max during the holidays and did not feel that he should be rewarded for this choice.

Initially, Nancy struggled to separate her feelings about James's choices from her vision of what she wanted for herself and Max moving forward. Her breakthrough came when she shifted her perspective: rather than focusing on what she felt James should have done differently or what she was missing out on, she began to consider what she truly wanted in her new life. For Nancy, that meant prioritizing a stable and positive environment for Max while still allowing him to feel connected to his extended family. By focusing on what she wanted for herself and her son rather than what she wanted from James, Nancy was able to move past resentment and make clearer decisions about their future.

IN THIS CHAPTER, you have set the stage for your divorce by understanding each person's background, choosing a supportive process, and engaging in transparent discovery. In the next chapter, I'll examine the "knots and traps" that can show up when unresolved emotions and repetitive conflict patterns in you and your spouse threaten to derail progress.

KEY TAKEAWAYS

- **Know your people:** Recognize that each person's unique background and emotional drivers influence the negotiation process.

- **Allow negotiations to unfold:** Embrace a gradual process that builds clarity and emotional space rather than one that rushes decisions.

- **Establish clear ground rules:** Set protocols for communication, decision-making, and confidentiality early to reduce misunderstandings.

- **Select the right process:** Choose among litigation, mediation, collaborative divorce, or negotiation based on your specific needs and dynamics.

- **Align with your lawyer:** Guide them with your true priorities. Speak up if their strategies clash with your long-term goals or values.

- **Commit to transparent information sharing:** Engage fully in discovery to ensure both parties have the complete facts needed for fair, informed decisions.

2

Navigating Knots and Traps

Have you ever found yourself in a conflict with someone, maybe your partner, where you feel stuck? Where you disagree but can't figure out why? If you find yourself in this situation, you might be thinking: if only your partner understood where you were coming from, there wouldn't be anything to fight about. To make matters worse, this fight has a pattern to it. The subject might change, but the result remains the same. I have a few recurring arguments with my husband, Richard, that land us in the same emotional quagmire every time. We've been to this place so many times that I could script out the conversation word for word, including how we both walk away feeling misunderstood and upset. I call this state of stuckness the *conflict trap*, and here is an example of how it might look in divorce.

Sarah called me about two years into her divorce process. She and her husband, Jerry, had been through a grueling negotiation. As Sarah described the situation, it sounded like she had gotten most of what she wanted, especially when it came to their three children. But there was still tension. Her voice was tight with frustration as she told me about their latest dispute: Jerry wanted a set of flowered towels that had been a gift to Sarah early in their marriage. She felt they were rightfully hers.

"Oh, Katherine," Sarah cried. "What do you think I should do?"

I paused. To Sarah, this fight seemed ridiculous—a stubborn, petty demand Jerry made just to get something from her. But I heard something else: Jerry felt out of control. Sarah had initiated the divorce and, with the court's help, secured primary custody of the children. The demand for the flowered towels wasn't so much about the towels; it was about Jerry salvaging some sense of control and dignity from a situation where he felt powerless.

"I think you should let him have the flowered towels," I replied gently.

There was silence on the other end of the phone, and then Sarah sighed. "You're right," she said quietly. We talked about how she could reframe the situation. She could buy herself new towels—flowered ones, if she liked—but by letting Jerry win this small battle, she could defuse the tension and preserve her energy for the bigger picture.

Sarah's struggle with Jerry wasn't unique—it was a classic example of the conflict trap. This term describes a pattern where small disagreements spiral into larger conflicts, fueled by reactions, counterreactions, and unaddressed emotions. The result? Both parties become entrenched in their positions, unable to see beyond the immediate argument.

When Sarah reframed this fight, she stepped out of the conflict trap. By recognizing that Jerry's demand was less about the flowered towels and more about his sense of dignity, she responded in a way that defused the situation rather than escalating it. But breaking free from this pattern isn't always easy, especially when emotions are high and the stakes feel enormous.

The Conflict Trap

In marriage, as in divorce, couples often develop entrenched patterns of conflict. These patterns, when left unresolved, resurface with new intensity during divorce negotiations.

Delia and Ethan, for example, came to mediation eager to work things out but found themselves locked in a familiar, frustrating cycle. Their arguments flared up with lightning speed, like a match to dry kindling. Delia would accuse Ethan of being irresponsible—whether about finances, parenting, or just remembering to pick up groceries. Ethan would respond with a biting remark about Delia being controlling and impossible to please. Before long each was entrenched in their position, replaying a script they had unknowingly memorized over years of marriage.

As their mediator, I could see the toll it was taking. Delia's frustration brimmed beneath her surface-level composure, while Ethan's shoulders sagged under the weight of what I suspected was his growing exhaustion. It wasn't just about the words they were saying in that moment; it was the deeper, unspoken history driving the fight—the years of hurt, resentment, and misunderstanding that had piled up between them.

When I paused the session to reflect back what I saw, there was an immediate shift in the room. I described their dynamic: how Delia's accusations seemed to come from a place of wanting to be heard, and how Ethan's defensiveness was his way of protecting himself from feeling inadequate. "It seems like you're both trying to connect, but instead you end up hurting each other," I said.

They sat in silence for a moment, and then Delia nodded. "That's exactly how it feels," she admitted, her voice softer now. Ethan glanced at her and added, "I don't want to hurt her—I just don't know what else to do when she comes at me like that."

For the first time, they weren't simply reacting to each other; they were seeing the dynamic that kept pulling them into conflict. By naming it, we externalized it and then turned it into something they could tackle together. It didn't fix everything overnight, but it gave them a starting point, a way to step out of the trap and start moving forward.

While the conflict trap reflects repetitive fights over surface issues, divorce is also the *emotional knot* that can keep you stuck unless you learn to focus on what truly matters.

The Emotional Knot of Divorce

Negotiating a divorce is like trying to untangle a knitting basket filled with yarn that a kitten has played in. Every thread—financial partnership, emotional history, parenting responsibilities, community ties—is intertwined with another. A fight about one issue—even a seemingly minor one, like flowered towels—can quickly spiral into a dispute about everything else, pulling on threads of resentment, loss, and fear. Withdrawing from a shared life, divorce becomes the untangling a complex emotional knot in which everything is connected: finances, identity, children, friendships, living arrangements...

Sorting through these threads requires patience, focus, and a willingness to separate what truly matters from what feels urgent in the moment. It's tempting to want immediate clarity, to try to solve everything at once. But attempting to untangle all the threads all at once will only pull the knots tighter. The key is to work with one thread at a time.

If you want to begin untangling the knots of your divorce, consider these steps:

- **Sort out the threads:** Identify what belongs where. Some decisions are financial, some emotional, and some relational—but often, a single thread carries more than one color. For example, keeping the house might seem like a financial issue, but it could also be tied to caring for an aging parent or preserving a sense of stability. Try not to let one category hijack another. If you're feeling deeply hurt about the end of the marriage, that pain may color how you approach financial decisions. Recognizing these overlaps can help you untangle what matters most in each decision—and prevent emotional triggers from becoming financial roadblocks.

- **Focus on what's in your control:** Some aspects of divorce will feel unfair, but fighting for perfect justice (unattainable in any human-made system) in every area will only add frustration. Shift your focus to what you can control: your choices, your mindset, and how you engage in the process.

- **Cut out the threads that don't matter:** Not everything needs to be fought over. Some things—like flowered towels—are best left alone, freeing your energy for what truly matters. If something is causing disproportionate stress, ask yourself: Do I need to hold on to this, or can I let it go?

- **Prioritize the future over the past:** The past will pull at you. Old wounds and grievances will surface. Acknowledging these feelings is important but letting them dictate your decisions keeps you stuck. Each decision in your divorce should include this question: Will this serve me and my family five years from now?

Divorce is an emotional transition as much as (or more than) it is a legal process. And like any complex transition, it requires *deliberate, step-by-step progress* rather than rushed, emotional reactions. With time, patience, and intention, the tangled threads will begin to separate.

The Three Levels of Conflict

Among the many brilliant things Albert Einstein said, one of them was, "We cannot solve our problems with the same thinking we used when we created them." This quote is often used in business to encourage creative problem-solving, but it's just as powerful in negotiation—especially divorce negotiations. Why? Because people rarely fight about the real problem—the root issue. Instead, they argue about the symptoms. This is why the best solutions often lie at a deeper level than the surface-level dispute.

If you want to break free from unproductive arguments, it helps to understand the *three levels of conflict* at play in any negotiation:

1. **Positions:** The surface-level demands. These are the *what* statements, like "I want the house," or "I want full custody."

2. **Interests:** The reasons behind those demands. These answer the *why*, like "I need stability," or "I want to protect my time with the kids."

3. **Meaning:** The emotional significance attached to the issue. These reflect the deeper fears and values, like "Losing the house feels like losing my role as a parent," or "Giving up custody feels like I'm losing my identity."

Let's take a closer look at each of these levels of conflict.

Positions

When we think of traditional bargaining, positions are the explicit demands or stances people take. For example, the car price is $X, or the salary offered is $Y. In divorce a position might be something like you can have the children every other weekend.

This type of positional bargaining is often two-dimensional, with each side presenting demands and attempting to persuade the other to concede. It's a win-lose framework: one party gets more only if the other gets less. If we stay stuck at this level, there are usually only three outcomes:

1. One person fully gives in to the other's position.
2. Both parties compromise, splitting the difference.
3. The negotiation breaks down altogether.

While compromise can seem like a reasonable solution—or what "good people" do in negotiation—it often fails to truly solve any underlying problem. A compromise may feel like progress, but it can leave both sides dissatisfied and the deeper issues unresolved.

Consider the classic example of two sisters arguing over the last orange. Their mother steps in to mediate and hears each girl insist, "I want the orange!" Frustrated, the mother might simply split the orange in half—a compromise. But neither girl is happy with that outcome because it doesn't solve either of their problems.

If the mother had asked why each sister wanted the orange, she might have discovered that one wanted the juice to soothe her sore throat while the other needed the rind to bake a cake—their interests. By understanding their interests rather than only their positions, the mother could have met both needs with the same orange. No compromise was necessary—just a deeper understanding of the problem.

If the orange story seems simple, you might wonder why we don't approach all negotiations this way. Three main reasons prevent us from digging deeper:

1. **Fear of vulnerability:** Sharing the real reasons behind your position—your interests—can feel risky. You might worry that revealing what's important to you will make you vulnerable to exploitation.

2. **Habit and instinct:** Many of us default to positions because they feel safer and clearer. Taking a position helps relieve the anxiety of uncertainty, giving us something to hold on to in a negotiation.

3. **Fear of being judged:** Expressing your deeper needs or concerns can feel exposing—not just because of potential consequences,

While compromise can seem like a reasonable solution—or what "good people" do in negotiation—it often fails to truly solve any underlying problem.

but because you fear being seen as unreasonable, emotional, or weak. This fear can keep you silent about what matters most, even when it's central to the outcome.

Staying at the level of positions can feel secure but often leads to frustration and impasse. It's like negotiating on a flat, horizontal plane, where each side tries to pull the other closer to their position without exploring the richer vertical dimension of interests and meaning.

Interests

Interests are the reasons behind the positions people take. They represent our hopes, fears, needs (such as security, stability, connection, autonomy, and dignity), and desires and are the *why* of negotiation. For instance, in the orange story I shared earlier, one sister needed orange juice to soothe her throat while the other sister wanted the orange rind for baking. Their interests revealed what each of them truly needed, and what was underlying their surface need for the orange.

Interestingly, in my experience, about 80 percent of interests in any divorce negotiation are shared between the parties. This means that even in conflict, there is significant common ground. However, identifying these interests requires curiosity and, often, vulnerability.

Take Marcy, whom I introduced earlier. When she first came to me, she was adamant about staying in her house. At first, it was hard for her to articulate why—it was a position that simply felt nonnegotiable. Over time, Marcy identified her underlying interests: she wanted stability for her children, to avoid the stress of moving, and to maintain her sense of security during a chaotic time. However, she also recognized conflicting concerns: the house was expensive and difficult to maintain and staying might not be the best decision long-term.

Once Marcy fully understood her interests, she realized that finding a new home—one that better suited her needs and financial reality—would provide greater stability for her family. Her clarity allowed her to move forward with confidence and prioritize what truly mattered.

Interests, not positions, are where the real work of negotiation happens. But there we also need explore below the level of interests and understand meaning.

Meaning

Meaning represents the deepest level of negotiation. It's about how people see themselves and their place in the world. Meaning connects to core values, identity, and the fundamental question: Who am I in the context of this conflict?

Divorce, as a profound life transition, often forces people to confront these deeper questions. It is a time of reorientation, one in which individuals grapple with what was and what will be. Negotiating at the level of meaning involves helping people align their choices with their true selves and values.

For years, Eric's identity was tied to his demanding career, which contributed to his divorce from Charlene. During negotiations, Eric initially insisted on maintaining his professional trajectory, prioritizing financial stability. But as discussions progressed, Eric reflected on what truly mattered to him. He realized that being an involved parent aligned more closely with his core values than his career. This shift allowed Eric to prioritize co-parenting arrangements over financial ambition, creating a resolution that honored both his needs and those of his family.

Charlene, however, found this shift bittersweet. While she supported Eric's increased involvement with their children, she couldn't ignore the resentment she felt—that it took the end of their marriage for him to recognize something she had long wished he would prioritize. Her experience is not uncommon: when one partner evolves only after the relationship breaks down, it can bring a complicated mix of relief, grief, and anger.

Exploring meaning in negotiation can make you feel vulnerable, but it is also empowering. When people connect with their core values, they often discover new possibilities and solutions that feel authentic and sustainable. Meaning moves negotiation beyond the transactional to the transformational, allowing both parties to emerge with outcomes that reflect their true selves.

When people argue about positions, they often miss the underlying interests and emotional meanings driving the conflict. And when these deeper layers are ignored, the conflict intensifies, leading to frustration, mistrust, and the feeling of being stuck. Let's go back to Sarah and Jerry and those flowered towels for a moment so I can show you the interplay of positions, interests, and meaning.

- **Position:** Jerry wanted the flowered towels. Sarah thought this was ridiculous, especially since the towels had been gifted to her.
- **Interest:** Jerry wanted to feel like he had some control in the divorce process.
- **Meaning:** At the deepest level, Jerry's insistence on the towels was about dignity. He felt powerless, and taking the towels was a symbolic way of asserting his worth.

When Sarah understood what was driving Jerry's demand, it transformed how she approached the situation. Letting go of the towels was not a loss—it was an opportunity for her to de-escalate the conflict and preserve her energy for what truly mattered.

This approach highlights an important principle: that true resolution requires a shift in perspective. As Einstein implied, if you stay at the surface level of conflict, you can't expect to find meaningful solutions. By understanding and addressing the deeper layers—interests and meaning—you can transform the negotiation process and create outcomes that reflect what truly matters to both parties.

When you understand the differences between positions, interests, and meaning, you can negotiate outcomes that go beyond compromise. Exploring interests allows us to uncover creative solutions, while addressing meaning ensures those solutions align with our values and identity. Divorce negotiations, though challenging, can become opportunities for clarity, connection, and growth when approached with curiosity and intention.

While recognizing and managing emotional triggers is essential, divorce also requires concrete decisions about daily life. This is where what I call the Big Three—parenting, asset division, and cash flow—come into play and are often the source of conflict traps and emotional knots. By shifting focus to these practical pillars, you can begin to anchor your negotiation in concrete decisions and forward momentum.

The Big Three

Divorce is complicated, multifaceted, and touches every part of your life—emotionally, financially, physically, and logistically. It challenges your sense of security and threatens the people, places, and things that you hold most dear. On top of that, the legal jargon and procedures can be confusing and frustrating, adding to the anxiety you may already feel about the future.

Breathe! There is good news: although divorce is complex, it's not insurmountable. Many of my clients come into the divorce process worried about keeping everything in their head. The key is to tackle one issue at a time, starting with the big-picture concerns and gradually working through the smaller details. It's important to acknowledge your emotions without letting them override the practical realities. Emotions can offer valuable insight into what matters most—but decisions that hold up over time are built on a foundation of both emotional truth and factual understanding. Along the way, it's perfectly normal for the plan to require some adjustments to make everything fit together smoothly. Now is the time to think about what issues are relevant to your situation. For most people, parenting (if you have children), dividing up your assets and liabilities, and figuring out how to pay the bills for yourselves and your family will be the key issues for you in a divorce. Whether you and your spouse come to an agreement on your own, with the assistance of a mediator or collaborative professional, or through the courts, the final divorce agreement will usually contain the same three essential pillars: a parenting plan, division of assets, and cash flow.

You will discuss the Big Three in depth with your lawyer or mediator but let me briefly describe how each of these pillars figure in your final divorce agreement.

Pillar #1: Parenting

No parent holds their newborn and thinks about *custody*. Instead, they think about love, responsibility, and their hopes for their child. As separated or divorced parents, the goal is to create a parenting plan that supports your child's well-being and development while ensuring both parents remain actively involved and the child has the benefit of the best each parent has to offer.

Parenting plans include two main components: *decision-making authority* and *time-sharing*.

1. **Decision-making authority** covers major issues such as medical care, education, and religious upbringing. Parents must decide if they will make these decisions jointly or if one parent will have final authority. Some parents divide responsibilities—one might handle education while the other oversees healthcare. Even in high-conflict cases, having a tie-breaking mechanism can prevent future disputes.

2. **Time-sharing** is a parenting plan that outlines when and where children will spend time with each parent. This includes both a regular schedule for weekdays and weekends as well as a special schedule for holidays, vacations, and birthdays. Even in an amicable situation, a basic schedule will eliminate the need for perpetual negotiations; you can work out exceptions to the regular arrangements when needed.

Balancing flexibility and reliability is key. Parents should create a schedule that considers their work commitments, children's needs, and each parent's ability to provide a stable environment.

Pillar #2: Division of Assets

Dividing marital property can be one of the most complex aspects of divorce. Understanding the difference between *marital property* and *separate property* is crucial.

- **Marital property**: Generally, assets acquired during the marriage, regardless of whose name is on the title although each state has its own definition.

- **Separate property:** Assets acquired before marriage, maybe inheritances and gifts from third parties, depending on your jurisdiction, and certain personal injury settlements. However, the classification of separate property can change depending on how it is handled during the marriage. For example, if separate property is *comingled*—such as by depositing inherited funds into a marital bank account—it may lose its separate status and be treated as marital property. Similarly, if a separate asset is retitled in both spouses' names, a court may consider it marital. These distinctions can be subtle and vary by state, so it's important to understand how your specific situation may be viewed under your local laws.

Your assets will also be divided differently according to the state you reside in. For example, in *equitable distribution* states, courts divide property based on a series of factors intended to guide the court to a fair determination and in consideration of factors such as length of the marriage, each spouse's financial contributions, further earning potential, and whether one spouse sacrificed career opportunities to care for children or to support the other's career. In *community property* states, however, marital assets are typically split fifty-fifty, although that is not true in every community property state, and in some community property states, separate property becomes community property under certain circumstances.

Examples of assets that can be divided include things such as real estate, bank and investment accounts, retirement funds and pensions, business interests, personal property (i.e., art, jewelry, vehicles), intellectual property, and cryptocurrency. Debt is also divided. Some debts are marital (such as mortgages or joint credit cards), while others (such as those incurred prior to the marriage) may remain separate. Prenuptial and postnuptial agreements clarify asset division before or during the marriage. However, they can be challenged in court if they are deemed unconscionable, signed under duress, or lack full financial disclosure without a proper waiver.

The last thing you need to know is that not all assets are equal when it comes to taxes. Some assets, like retirement accounts, stock options, and investment properties, may come with capital gains taxes or early withdrawal penalties. When dividing assets, it's important to consider not just their face value but also their after-tax value.

Asset division, and their tax implications, can be complex, so please work with your lawyer or an accountant to ensure you understand your unique situation.

Pillar #3: Cash Flow

Divorce isn't just about dividing assets—it's also about ensuring financial stability moving forward. Cash flow focuses on how each new household will support themselves after divorce. The key financial considerations when it comes to your cash flow are

- **Spousal support** (also called alimony, maintenance, or post-divorce support) is support from one spouse to the other based on financial need and earning capacity.
- **Basic child support** covers children's essential needs (housing, food, clothing).
- **Add-on child support** covers expenses like medical costs, extracurricular activities, and education.

It's important to know that courts may *impute income* to a spouse who is unemployed or underemployed, meaning they calculate *potential* earnings rather than *actual* income to determine support obligations.

Think of your post-divorce financial plan as building a house:

- **Foundation:** your immediate expenses (housing, food, utilities).
- **Structure:** future financial shifts (children's growth, job changes, inflation).
- **Roof:** your long-term financial stability (retirement, asset distribution).

Instead of focusing on every possible worst-case scenario, I like to recommend that you start with *what is likely* and build in flexibility for life's inevitable changes. And, as with asset division, there may be tax implications to be aware of when it comes to cash flow. Please consult with your lawyer or an accountant to be certain you understand your obligations no matter what side of the table you are on.

THESE THREE major pillars will form the foundation of your divorce agreement—and are usually supported by smaller topics that round out the full plan. You may find yourself falling into conflict traps as you work through the Big Three in your negotiations. It's not always easy to determine what needs to be negotiated and what is a distraction. Allen and Grace's story provides a helpful lens through which to understand how focusing on the Big Three can untangle the complexities of divorce, even in a highly charged and emotional situation.

Allen and Grace: A Story of Complexity

Allen and Grace had been married for several decades and they had two children, one in college and one in high school. Allen had retired early after a successful career as an attorney and founded a charity focused on social justice that he and Grace worked on together. He made a decent salary from the charity, and Grace a smaller one, but their lifestyle was largely funded by income from investments. Together they owned a primary home as well as a lake house. Grace's good friend Joanne and her husband also had a lake house nearby, and the two couples had enjoyed many evenings together out of town.

Like many couples, Allen and Grace had trouble communicating intimately, so they had been in couples counseling for years. But one weekend, Allen found himself confiding in Joanne and felt heard by her in a way that he had not felt from Grace in many years. One thing led to another, and Allen and Joanne fell in love.

Eventually, in a session with their therapist, Allen told Grace about his feelings for Joanne and indicated that he wanted to separate from Grace on a trial basis to find out if the relationship with Joanne was viable. Grace was devastated. She was hurt and angry that Allen wanted to separate, but that he was leaving with her best

Instead of focusing on every possible worst-case scenario, start with *what is likely* and build in flexibility for life's inevitable changes.

friend was an intolerable betrayal. And when Grace told their children what had happened between Allen and Joanne, they were hurt and angered as well. The whole family was in crisis.

In the midst of this emotional storm, Grace met with her lawyer, who encouraged her to focus on practical decisions despite her feelings. They began by addressing the first pillar: parenting. Grace had been the primary caregiver throughout the marriage, but Allen had always been an involved father and an important part of their children's lives. Realizing that their children's well-being was the top priority, Grace agreed to develop a parenting plan for the minor children that would maintain Allen's role in their lives while giving the children space to process their emotions. They decided on a flexible schedule that respected the children's wishes but also encouraged gradual rebuilding of their relationship with their father. This wasn't easy for Grace, who felt that Allen did not deserve to continue to interact with the children, but she was able to sort out what she ultimately realized was best for them in the long run. While custody agreements legally apply only to children under eighteen, older children can still benefit from parental guidance about what both parents agree is appropriate. This helps ensure that one parent isn't unfairly burdened or alienated simply because the children hold them responsible for enforcing limits. Next, they looked at the second pillar: division of assets. Although Grace's initial reaction was to make Allen pay for his actions by demanding the lake house and the majority of their investments, her lawyer reminded her that focusing on punishment would not necessarily lead to a sustainable agreement. They discussed the long-term implications of the asset division, including the cost of maintaining the lake house and the need for consistent cash flow post-divorce. After a series of discussions, Grace agreed that selling the lake house and splitting the proceeds would allow both parties to move forward without being tied to a painful memory.

Finally, they addressed the third pillar: cash flow. Grace was concerned about maintaining her standard of living, especially since her income from the charity was minimal compared to Allen's earnings.

Allen, on the other hand, did not want to disrupt the charity's operations or jeopardize his own financial stability. After discussing their budgets and projected needs, they settled on a spousal and child support arrangement that provided Grace with enough stability and also allowed Allen to maintain his investment strategies.

Through these negotiations, Grace learned to distinguish between her desire to make Allen feel the pain she felt and her genuine need for financial security and a stable environment for the children. Gradually, by focusing on the Big Three pillars of parenting, asset division, and cash flow, Grace and Allen were able to create a comprehensive divorce agreement. Although the emotional wounds took time to heal, the couple's ability to separate feelings from practical decisions helped them move forward in a way that preserved their children's well-being and their own financial stability. Grace's shifting focus from what she wanted from Allen to what she wanted for her new life was key to breaking free from the conflict trap.

Allen and Grace's story illustrates how the practical challenges of divorce—parenting arrangements, financial support, and division of assets—are often complicated by conflicting emotions. In Grace's case, the pain of a double betrayal and the reactive wish for retribution clashed with her desire to prioritize their children's well-being. To move forward, Grace had to sort through where each of these feelings was coming from and understand how to use them to make thoughtful, balanced decisions.

Finding Your Way Through the Maze

Conflict traps and emotional knots can make a divorce negotiation so much a maze of emotions, logistics, and legal decisions that you don't even know where to start. This is why so many people stay stuck—either in endless conflict or in avoidance—hoping things will sort themselves out. But the key to navigating the maze of divorce is recognizing what truly matters and focusing your energy where it will make the biggest impact. The only way forward is to separate what is urgent from what is important. Ask yourself the following questions:

- Am I fighting about this issue because it truly matters? Or is it tied to deeper emotions that need to be processed separately for me to move forward?

- What are the real priorities in this divorce? What will matter to me and my family five years from now? It can be useful to think about how you want your children to look back on how both parents managed to care for them through the divorce process.

- How can I shift my focus from positions (what I want) to interests (why it matters) and ultimately to meaning (what this says about who I am and what I value)?

At the same time, divorce touches on every aspect of your life—finances, identity, children, and community—making it overwhelming to sort out what truly matters. Without clarity, it's easy to remain stuck in positions instead of uncovering the interests and meaning that can lead to resolution. But when you move beyond reactive conflict and address the real issues—whether they involve parenting, financial security, or redefining your future—you take control of the process rather than letting it control you.

RECOGNIZING PATTERNS of conflict and emotion is an important first step, but awareness alone isn't enough. To truly move forward, you have to make intentional choices about how you engage in the process. That means deciding which battles are worth fighting, acknowledging the emotions driving your reactions, and focusing on outcomes that serve your long-term well-being.

By shifting from a reactive mindset to a strategic one, you create space for solutions rather than remaining trapped in frustration and emotional entanglement. So, in the next chapter, I'll explore how to chart your own emotional journey during the divorce process that will lead to resolution rather than gridlock.

KEY TAKEAWAYS

- **The conflict trap keeps you stuck:** Repetitive fights reflect old patterns. Recognizing them helps you shift focus to what truly matters.

- **Divorce is an emotional knot:** Untangle one thread at a time, prioritizing what's most important for the future.

- **Not everything is worth fighting for:** Ask if a battle will matter in five years, then focus on your genuine needs and long-term goals.

- **Go deeper than positions:** Understanding the *why* (interests) and *who* (meaning) behind demands opens the door to creative solutions.

- **The Big Three matter:** Parenting, asset division, and cash flow form the core pillars of divorce negotiation; addressing them systematically helps reduce your overwhelm and keep priorities clear.

- **Focus on real issues, and navigate with intention:** Clarify long-term goals like stability, financial security, and co-parenting to reduce emotional roadblocks.

3

Charting Your Emotional Divorce Journey

MATTHEW WAS miserable in his marriage. He and his wife had been living apart for over a year, and he wanted to formalize their separation and create some financial guidelines and a parenting plan so he could spend time with their three kids. But here he was, in my office, telling me that he was not the kind of guy who gets divorced. Matthew found himself in an emotional box, wanting out but not wanting to be "that guy." Ultimately, Matthew decided to divorce but to do it in a way where he felt that he was still taking care of his family and treating his ex with respect, even though he was very angry at her.

Beginning the divorce process can feel like stepping into an emotional whirlwind—one filled with uncertainty, fear, sadness, and even moments of relief. This mix of emotions is entirely normal, and taking the time to understand them will help guide you through the practical steps ahead. In fact, it's crucial to the success of your divorce negotiation.

What You Might Be Thinking

In the early stages of a divorce you are probably doing more feeling than thinking. But when you are thinking you're probably thinking about solutions that would work for you. This can sound something like, "Well, if I have to be divorced, then at least I'm not going to make my children move." Your solution to this situation might be to keep the family home whether you live in it or not.

Thinking about solutions is a common and natural response to the anxiety you might experience, especially as you don't know what's going to happen. Although solution thinking can help you figure out what is most important to you, keep in mind that despite the early appeal of a quick or one-sided resolution, some ideas may not turn out to be as good as they seemed.

You might believe that holding on to the home is the single most important thing because it won't physically disrupt the lives of your children (or the life of one partner). However, later on, it may turn out that the home is too expensive or too much work to keep up. Still, knowing that you *want* to hold on to the home gives you the opportunity to explore why that is important to you. Is it about not wanting to hurt the children or disrupt their lives more than necessary? Or is it about security or appearances? One way to clarify your thoughts is to make a list of what you *think* you want, ask yourself why that is, and write down your answers for each want on your list.

At this time, you are probably also thinking that you need to protect yourself and hire a good lawyer. No doubt you're wondering how to find the best one for you. Here's where your thinking may be misguided. Yes, you should hire a good lawyer. But contrary to every billboard you might see along your local interstate, a lawyer who promises to fight for you may not be the right fit for your situation.

Depending on your goals, hiring a lawyer with mediation skills (or hiring a mediator) or one who has collaborative or negotiation skills might be better than the traditional fighter-type. Think about adopting a more holistic approach—your divorce is more than just the numbers. Allow yourself to include considerations about your emotional and psychological well-being and those people you care about.

What You Might Be Feeling

Divorce isn't simply a legal or financial matter; it's a deeply personal and emotionally charged process. Even though you may be thinking about solutions or the next steps, this is also the time to take a step back and recognize the feelings that come with such a major life change. The decision to divorce is one of the hardest you will ever make and is never without doubt or confusion. And if the divorce is not your choice, it can be even harder. But what you need to know is that your feelings play a critical role in how you approach your decisions and negotiations.

You may be scattered and unsure of what you do truly feel. This disorienting feeling comes from a mixture of common competing emotions ranging from sadness, anger, disappointment, and relief to fear, embarrassment, guilt, and shame. Throw a bit of excitement and powerlessness to the mix, and you have a potent emotional cocktail. You are not alone! My clients experience all of these feelings, and this can lead to an exhaustion and turmoil. That's part of what makes the decision to divorce so challenging. Understanding what you're feeling will provide clarity and help you make more thoughtful and informed choices as you move forward. As I explore some of the reasons for why you might feel the way you do, take some time to consider which of the following emotions you're experiencing right now:

- **Anger:** By the time people decide to divorce, they are often feeling outraged by the behavior or attitude of their ex. If there was an affair or other betrayal that led to the decision to divorce, it's not uncommon for the betrayed person to feel at once powerless and vengeful. Watch out for anger; outrage and self-righteousness can become a slippery slope toward making bad decisions.

- **Hurt:** Underneath anger, there's often hurt—a feeling of emotional injury that comes from being let down, rejected, or betrayed. You may feel wounded by the way your spouse treated you or by how the relationship turned out despite your efforts. This kind of pain can be hard to acknowledge because it leaves you feeling exposed and vulnerable. But recognizing the hurt, rather than covering it with blame or shutting it down, can be a powerful step toward healing.

- **Sadness:** Anger is often the outer skin of sadness. The life you planned is ending. The wishes, hopes, and dreams you had about your marriage, your family, and your home are not to be, so it's not surprising you will feel sad about this perceived loss. If you're overwhelmed by this emotion, seek professional help to get you through the transition.

- **Guilt:** When someone decides to end a marriage, whether as a result of an affair—fully consummated or not—or for some other reason, this usually creates some feelings of guilt. Guilt is a big factor in the psychology of divorce negotiation; if you or the other party seeks to take advantage of guilt in your negotiations, that guilt can quickly turn to anger.

- **Shame:** A powerful emotion that can drive us to extreme behavior, shame often arises in the wake of divorce—not just because of the relationship itself but because of what the end of the marriage seems to *represent*. For some, the shame comes from how divorce is reshaping their identity, lifestyle, or social standing. For others, it stems from their ex's behavior during the marriage—or from their own. And sometimes, shame is rooted in long-standing messages from family or culture: beliefs about failure, commitment, or what a "good" marriage or person should look like. Regardless of its source, shame is rarely helpful—and it must be acknowledged and addressed or it can quietly sabotage your ability to heal, make sound decisions, or move forward.

- **Relief:** When people have tried for years to make their marriage work, perhaps if only for the sake of their children, they may experience a sense of relief when the decision to divorce is finally made. Ironically, the decision to divorce can create such a release for a couple that they get along much better than they have for years.

What makes this stew of emotions even more potent is that they can cycle randomly, much like the stages of grief do, disorienting you. One moment you are experiencing a sense of relief, the next you are overcome with anger. It can be unnerving when your feelings shift rapidly, but this is a natural part of the emotional process of divorce. Allowing yourself the space to feel all of these emotions without judgment can help you move forward in a healthier way. Keep in mind that all these feelings contain valuable information. Figuring out how to mine that information is a crucial part of the divorce negotiation process; I'll talk more about how to do this later in part two of this book.

Clarify Your Goals

Many of my clients feel lost in these early stages of divorce, wrestling with conflicting emotions. But this confusion doesn't last forever—it's simply the starting point before gaining clarity. Divorce can be a bitter pill to swallow regardless of whether you are the person ending the marriage or the decision to divorce is made by your spouse and there is nothing you can do to change it. The cocktail of emotions associated with both these scenarios is discombobulating. But knowing what you want is crucial. Take the examples of Oscar and Geri and of Meg and Paul.

Oscar was a successful pharmaceutical salesman whose marriage to Geri was on the rocks. He described his role in his marriage as that of the provider, but he felt entirely unappreciated. He would come home late from work, and no one would eat dinner with him. He wanted more and found it in a relationship with Sandra.

Unfortunately, Geri heard about the about the relationship between Oscar and Sandra at a Christmas party, and she was angry, hurt, and embarrassed. In retaliation, Geri told everyone she could think of, including the couple's four children, that Oscar was a lying, cheating, good-for-nothing. Oscar was devastated, his children wouldn't talk to him, and his world was collapsing. But intuitively he felt that even though the situation was painful, and he did not know what the future held, that things could be different for him and that he would grow through the experience.

Oscar experienced a disorienting mess of conflicting thoughts and emotions throughout his divorce. He had a strong moral ethic that applied to his family and to his work. There were things he thought a person should do and things they shouldn't do. Divorce and an extramarital relationship were not on his "should do" list. And yet, the relationship with Sandra made him happy. After Oscar settled his divorce with Geri, he married Sandra. His children saw the transformation in their dad, and ultimately ended up spending a great deal of time with him and Sandra at their home.

Geri, on the other hand, struggled to move past the anger and betrayal she felt. For a long time, she remained stuck in her feelings of resentment, convinced that Oscar's choices had ruined not only their marriage but also her sense of stability. It wasn't until her oldest daughter approached her one evening, expressing how torn she felt between her parents, that Geri began to reconsider how her own reaction was impacting her children.

Slowly, Geri started to focus on what she truly wanted moving forward. She didn't want to be defined by anger or stuck in the past. Instead, she wanted to reclaim her sense of self and create a new life that wasn't centered on her disappointment in Oscar. Through therapy and self-reflection, Geri found a way to balance her pain with the desire to build something positive for herself and her children.

Over time, Geri was able to redefine her role within her family and regain a sense of purpose. She even began to let go of her bitterness toward Oscar, realizing that holding on to it was keeping her from moving on. In the end, Geri's journey was about rediscovering her own strength and recognizing that her happiness didn't have to be tied to her marriage or to Oscar's choices.

Meg and Paul found themselves in a slightly different situation. Meg had been married to Paul for almost two decades. Their active family of five kept them busy and exhausted. When I met with Meg, she wasn't sure when the last time was that she and Paul had sex, but she was certain it hadn't been for several years. One Saturday

Paul asked her to go for coffee, and he told her that he felt like they were roommates and he wanted to find a relationship that provided emotional intimacy. While Paul wanted to be friendly and amicable with Meg, he no longer wanted to be in a marriage with her and had been dating several other women.

Meg was surprised and shocked. She told me that she knew their relationship wasn't great, but she didn't think it was bad enough to divorce. "He didn't even ask to go to therapy," she said through sobs. "I thought we'd figure it out or get divorced when the kids were gone." Meg also found herself disoriented and confused. She couldn't really blame Paul for wanting something more. In fact, she had often contemplated how nice it would be to feel like she had an intimate relationship with her partner. But she was definitely hurt and angry that Paul had concluded their marriage had no potential without discussing it with her first. And she initially carried that anger into their divorce negotiation until she figured out that it was harming her ability to see things clearly.

With the help of her attorney and a good divorce coach, Meg was able to gradually let go of her resentment and to approach the negotiations with a clearer sense of purpose. She realized that she was angry because Paul's decision threatened her sense of security, for herself and their three kids, but that her unhappiness in the marriage was endangering her overall well-being. Through the negotiations, Meg realized that she could have a new kind of stability and the possibility for a truly intimate relationship.

One day, as Meg sat in her cozy new apartment, she caught herself smiling. She had spent the afternoon painting—something she hadn't done in years—and it struck her how light and free she felt. There was no one to judge how she spent her time, no unspoken resentment lingering in the air. For the first time in decades, she felt like herself. Meg saw real potential in her new life. She began to explore new friendships, tried dating tentatively, and discovered a passion for hiking that gave her a sense of adventure and clarity. She and Paul worked hard to maintain a cooperative relationship for the sake of their children, and she found, to her surprise, they now got along better than they had in years.

Understanding who your spouse or partner cares about may seem like an unnecessary or even painful exercise when your emotions are running high, but this insight can be a powerful tool in negotiations.

YOU MIGHT be grappling with conflicting emotions, unsure of how to move forward. Maybe some of the experiences of the couples I've just talked about feel familiar to you. Maybe you have your own curious mixture of feelings, thoughts, and impulses.

But in all of that emotional stew, understanding what is important to you and why is crucial to negotiating a good outcome in your divorce. To gain this clarity, I like to guide my clients through a two-part exercise that encourages them to think deeply about what matters most—not only to them but to their ex and the others involved.

Understanding who your spouse or partner cares about may seem like an unnecessary or even painful exercise when your emotions are running high, but this insight can be a powerful tool in negotiations. If you can recognize where their priorities lie, this may reveal areas where compromises can be made, leading to solutions that ultimately serve both your interests.

The next section offers you a two-part questioning exercise to work through this more substantively.

An Exercise in Understanding

Who Do You Care About?
In this first part of the exercise, you will ask yourself: *Who are the people who matter to me?*

If you have children, they are probably on the list. What about your family of origin: your parents, siblings, and extended family—maybe even your in-laws? Now think about your friends, neighbors, co-workers and colleagues, or spiritual community. Who gets to be on your list? Write out those names and be honest because this list is just for you.

Now, ask yourself: *Who are the people who matter to my ex?*

If you are feeling angry or bitter, you might need someone to help you work through this list. The truth is, if you let yourself think about the answer to this question without dipping into judgment, you probably have a good understanding of who matters to your former spouse or partner. Work through the same lists I mentioned in the first question: family, friends, community, co-workers and colleagues, spiritual community, and so on.

What Do You Care About?

I recommend you do this second part of the exercise with a trusted friend or family member, if not with your lawyer or therapist. You need to feel safe to do it well, and it is probably easier to do with a trusted support person.

The other trick with this exercise is to avoid negativity—something our brains are wired for. As neuropsychologist Dr. Rick Hanson writes in his blog, "The mind is like Velcro for negative experiences and Teflon for positive ones." Though this so-called "negativity effect" might have worked well for our Paleolithic ancestors, it doesn't work at all in our current situation.

You are building a future you want—your future—one that is going to impact the kind of parent you are, the lifestyle you lead, and your happiness. To counteract the negativity bias as you work through this second part of the exercise, try asking yourself: *What opportunities could this change bring?* Shifting your focus to potential positives, even in difficult circumstances, helps you start building the future you truly want.

Are you ready? In this part of the exercise I want you to think intentionally about what you want in the following four steps:

Step 1: Think deeply about *what* you care about. Write down what you care about in each of the following areas:

- personal
- financial
- relationships
- family
- time/other

Step 2: Now, ask yourself *why* you care about these things. For example, if you wrote down "I want to stay in my house," ask yourself why. Do you feel overwhelmed and can't imagine having to move right now? Are you worried about uprooting your children and making them bear the consequences of their parents' decision to divorce? Do you want to keep the children in the local school? Do you like the neighbors? Does the house seem like a solid and safe financial asset? What else might be going on for you?

Step 3: Next, think through what your ex cares about in the same areas. If your ex has a new relationship, you might be thinking that perhaps that is all she or he cares about at the moment. But as with the first part of this exercise, if you avoid judgment, you probably have a good idea what your ex cares about. And it's likely that the new relationship is only one thing on that list.

Step 4: Finally, make sure to put yourself on the list! Ask yourself what being on your own list would mean. What decisions would you make differently if you prioritized your own well-being alongside that of others?

LET ME offer you an example of how this questioning exercise worked for Marcy, whom I have been talking about throughout.

Marcy's Lists

Marcy was committed to staying in her house when she first came to see me. She had just learned about Steve's affair, and the idea that she would lose not only her marriage partner and her sense of family but also her home while at the same time disrupting her kids through no fault of theirs was... well, it was not going to happen! She was adamant that her life shouldn't change (that much) because Steve had decided to break their vows.

Of course, Marcy was heartbroken and scared. She was afraid she would have to move back to her hometown in order to be able to afford a reasonable lifestyle. She was ashamed about having to tell the neighbors, her friends, and the nanny. She wanted to keep everything in her life as intact as possible and that included staying in the family house.

First, I asked her to complete the exercise about who she cared about. She made the following list of people she cares about:

- her children, Harrison and Emma (they were at the top of the list, with a big exclamation point!)
- her parents and her sisters
- neighbors who had also become her good friends
- her in-laws; especially her in sister-in-law, with whom she had a close relationship and who was Harrison's godmother

To a lesser extent, she also cared about the nanny, the other parents at the school, the teachers, and Steve's co-workers, with whom they had frequently socialized.

As we reviewed the worksheet for this part of the exercise, I congratulated Marcy on her thoughtfulness. Then she said, "You know, Katherine, I care a lot about me too. I should be on this list as well!" That was a terrific insight on Marcy's part (and how it got added as the fourth step in my exercise).

For the next step, I asked Marcy to think through what she cared about and why. "Well, I want to stay in the house," she said. I asked her to think through exactly what staying in the house did for her. "I'm not saying that you won't stay in the house or that it is not a good idea for you to do that," I assured her. "I want to understand more about why you feel so strongly about it to make sure that we are working toward a result that reinforces those goals." I'm not sure that she believed me at the time, but she took the worksheets and promised to work on them. (You can find this worksheet template online at katherinemiller.com/savvydivorce/worksheet.)

This is what Marcy brought back two weeks later when we met to prepare for a joint meeting with Steve and his lawyer.

Charting Your Emotional Divorce Journey 67

	Mine What do I care about?	**My Spouse's** If I were in their shoes, what would I care or worry about?	**Others'** What are the concerns of others who may be significantly affected?
Personal	Career—establishing a professional identity Being a good mom and role model for my kids Ultimately having a successful partnership	Maintain my professional reputation Have common interests with my partner Continue to grow career	My family and in-laws: minimize weirdness
Financial	A sustainable budget Financial independence Secure financial future Maintain or grow business	Be able to live well Maintain my lifestyle Workable budget Protect partnership	
Relationships	Available mother Good co-parenting relationship with Steve Continue to feel a part of my community	Good co-parenting relationship with Marcy Maintain friendships	Friends and neighbors: guidance on how to be friends with Marcy and Steve

	Mine What do I care about?	**My Spouse's** If I were in their shoes, what would I care or worry about?	**Others'** What are the concerns of others who may be significantly affected?
Family	Continuity for my family Emotional support for me and the kids Steve and I make great co-parents and can spend time together with the kids	Be a dad in a significant way Include new partner in family events Stability for the kids	Kids: have a mom and dad who are in our lives My family and in-laws: keep family involvement
Time / Other	Connection to some intellectual pursuit/ further education Flexible schedule Time to go to yoga / for self-care		

When Marcy brought in her notes in for our meeting, she remarked that this had been a powerful exercise for her. "Steve is not a bad guy," she said. "In some ways, I don't blame him for the affair because we have grown apart. I wish that I had kept up with my career or at least my friends from my days working in publishing. It's as if he had a whole life separate from me and the kids, and this affair is part of that. I'm angry with him and hurt, but in some weird way, I also understand. This exercise helped me gain some perspective."

When Marcy entered her divorce negotiation with Steve, this emotional clarity gave her the confidence to negotiate from a position of self-awareness. She could now articulate her needs clearly and recognize areas where Steve's concerns overlapped with her own, which paved the way for a more amicable discussion.

The exercise of thinking through who was important and what was important and why gave Marcy the chance to really examine her thoughts and feelings and think about who she is and what really matters to her. This is the grounded place I want you to be in when you start your divorce negotiations.

BY TAKING the time to reflect on what truly matters to you—especially what you are feeling and thinking—and recognizing that your spouse or partner has their own perspective, you are building a foundation for a future that reflects your values. Divorce may be one of life's hardest challenges, but with clarity and intention, you can navigate it in a way that leaves you stronger and more aligned with your true self.

However, one thing that can block you from accessing your true emotions in a helpful way is anxiety. At first, anxiety can be a signpost that something is making you uneasy. But after that its usefulness dissipates and anxiety becomes an impediment to negotiation. In the next chapter, I want to talk about how anxiety gets in the way of getting the best results and offer you some strategies on how to turn that around.

KEY TAKEAWAYS

- **Emotions are signals:** Acknowledge anger, hurt, sadness, guilt, shame, and relief as cues, not barriers, to your deeper needs.

- **Identify your priorities:** Clarify who and what matter most—like your children, your well-being, and your values—so you negotiate from a stable place.

- **Consider your ex's viewpoint:** Understanding their concerns can reveal common ground and collaborative solutions.

- **Combat the negativity bias:** Our minds are wired to focus on the negative, but shifting your attention to potential opportunities allows you to envision a brighter future.

- **Stay open to growth:** Overcome negativity bias, reflect on your experiences, and see divorce as an opportunity to reimagine your future.

4

Anxiety Gets in the Way

IT WASN'T UNTIL I was in my forties that I learned anxiety wouldn't kill me—but it sure felt like it might. The deep discomfort of anxiety often led me to search for a quick solution so that I could stop feeling anxious as quickly as possible. The problem was that the fastest solution was usually not the best. Anxiety makes us afraid, and it's hard to make the best decisions when you are fearful. If I had tolerated the anxiety a little longer, likely I would have made better or more productive decisions.

Divorce negotiations are fertile ground for anxiety as uncertainty about the future can quickly spiral into a need to act. David's story illustrates how destructive anxiety can be when it drives your decision-making:

> When my ex-wife and I were negotiating the division of our assets, I felt an overwhelming sense of anxiety. I was worried about my financial future and the potential loss of our family home. I was really worried about the kids and thought that they should stay in the home no matter what. Every time I thought about the uncertainty and the possible outcomes, my anxiety would skyrocket.
>
> One day, during a particularly stressful negotiation meeting, my anxiety hit an all-time high. I just wanted the stress to end. I

couldn't stand the uncertainty and the tension anymore. So, when my ex-wife's lawyer proposed a settlement, I hastily agreed to it without fully considering the consequences. The settlement heavily favored my ex-wife and left me with minimal financial security and no claim to our family home. My lawyer tried to stop me from agreeing, but I just couldn't hear her through the roar of pain in my head.

Agreeing to that unfavorable settlement put me in a tough financial spot. I found myself struggling to make ends meet, and the stress only escalated. Worse, losing access to the family home was emotionally devastating. It was a place filled with memories and significance, and now I felt displaced and regretful.

Afterwards, I realized that I acted out of desperation to stop my anxiety rather than making a well-considered choice. I was angry and frustrated with myself for not seeking better advice or taking more time to think things through. The need for immediate relief led to long-term negative consequences.

In hindsight David told me that he wished he had sought help with his anxiety during the divorce.

Anxiety is a function of our brain trying to help us, but instead of making us safer, it often makes things worse. So what exactly is it? According to the American Psychological Association, anxiety is an emotion characterized by feelings of tension and worry, and physical changes like increased blood pressure. Anxiety is often characterized by a constant apprehension about things we cannot control in the future. Although anxiety may feel like fear, fear is an immediate and short-lived response to a clearly identifiable and specific threat. *Psychology Dictionary* defines *fright* as "the emotional reaction that arises in the face of a dangerous or potentially dangerous situation or encounter." Anxiety is different from fear because it is diffuse, unspecific, and unsolvable. It is closely linked to the body's fight, flight, or freeze response, a physiological reaction to perceived threats. This behavioral response is a survival mechanism of the brain that prepares the body to either confront or avoid danger in various ways.

- **Perception of threat:** Anxiety often begins with the perception of a threat, whether real or imagined. This could be a stressful situation, an upcoming event, or even intrusive thoughts. There are plenty of perceived threats in divorce—some of which may even be quite real. The irony is that it is hard to see the real threats when anxiety clouds your view.

- **Activation of the amygdala:** The amygdala, a part of the brain involved in processing emotions, detects the threat and sends signals to other parts of the brain and body to prepare for a response.

- **Release of stress hormones:** The hypothalamus activates the autonomic nervous system, leading to the release of stress hormones like adrenaline and cortisol from the adrenal glands.

- **Physiological changes:** These hormones cause various physiological changes, such as increased heart rate, rapid breathing, muscle tension, and heightened alertness. These changes are part of the fight, flight, or freeze response.

- **Behavioral response:** Depending on the individual's predisposition and the context, they may exhibit fight, flight, or freeze behaviors. For example, someone might lash out (fight), avoid the situation (flight), or feel unable to move or speak (freeze).

When anxiety takes over, our natural instincts can make productive negotiations nearly impossible. Psychologist Daniel Goleman coined the term *amygdala hijack* in his 1995 book *Emotional Intelligence* to describe this phenomenon—when the brain's emotional center overrides the rational brain, triggering fight, flight, or freeze responses. Understanding these reactions can help you pause, regain control, and avoid making decisions you'll later regret.

Now, let's explore those three responses and take a closer look at how they might manifest in a divorce negotiation.

Fight Response

This response prepares the body to confront a threat. It can manifest as increased aggression, irritability, or a heightened sense of alertness. The body releases adrenaline and other stress hormones, which increases heart rate, blood pressure, and muscle tension, preparing a person to defend themselves.

In a divorce negotiation, this manifests as constant arguing, putting the other person down, and competition over every element—a win-lose paradigm but with no winners. Here's what it looks and sounds like:

Jane and Tom are in the middle of divorce negotiations. Jane is particularly anxious about the division of assets and the custody arrangement for their two children. She fears losing her financial stability and not being able to see her children as often as she would like.

During a mediation session, Tom proposes a custody arrangement that Jane perceives as unfavorable. She immediately feels a surge of anxiety, triggering her fight response. Jane leans forward in her chair, her body tense and her eyes narrowed. She interrupts the mediator, raising her voice: "This is completely unacceptable! I won't let you take my children away from me!"

Her language becomes more aggressive and confrontational as she directs her frustration toward Tom and the mediator. "Tom, you're trying to paint me as a bad mother! That's not going to happen. You're the one who's never around, always working late. I've been the one raising our kids!"

Jane becomes inflexible and refuses to consider any alternative proposals. Her anxiety and the fight response make her focus on defending her position rather than finding a middle ground. "I demand full custody, and I want the house. I'm not going to settle for anything less!"

In her heightened state of anxiety, Jane begins to make personal attacks, which escalate the tension in the room. "This whole situation is your fault, Tom!" she says. "You never cared about this family. All you care about is yourself and your job!"

Jane's fight response, driven by her anxiety, disrupts the negotiation process. Her aggressive stance and unwillingness to compromise lead to increased conflict and make it difficult for both parties to reach an agreement. This response can also cause emotional harm, and it strains the co-parenting relationship that is crucial for their children's well-being. Her hurtful words cannot be unsaid.

In reality, Jane is terrified. Inside, she cannot believe she is acting this way. What she really wants is a co-parenting arrangement with Tom where they can share responsibility and time in a cooperative way. But she feels personally at risk, and she is terribly anxious about how she will feel about herself when the children are with Tom and the house is empty. What will she do with that time? Does it make her a bad mother that she won't be with the children at all times? Jane wants to feel confident and more at peace in this new relationship with Tom, but instead she finds herself acting angrily and irrationally. She is annoyed with herself and upset with the mediator for allowing this to happen.

Flight Response

This response gears the body to escape from danger. It can cause a person to feel restless, jittery, or compelled to flee a situation. Physiological changes include increased breathing rate to supply more oxygen to the muscles, faster heartbeat, and a surge of energy, all aimed at facilitating quick movement away from the threat.

In divorce negotiations, this often makes someone unwilling to talk. They make it impossible to schedule meetings and refuse to share information about what their real needs are. Here's what it looks and sounds like:

Michael and Laura are in the process of negotiating their divorce settlement. Michael is particularly anxious about the financial aspects of the divorce, fearing that he may end up with a significant financial burden and less time with his children.

During a negotiation meeting, Laura's attorney suggests a financial settlement that Michael finds overwhelming and unfair. The anxiety triggers his flight response. Michael starts to physically pull back, leaning away from the table and avoiding eye contact with Laura and the lawyers. He fidgets with his pen, looks down at his papers, and appears distracted.

Michael becomes increasingly silent and unresponsive, avoiding participation in the discussion. When asked for his opinion or response, he mutters short, noncommittal answers like "I don't know" or "I need more time." The pressure and anxiety make Michael want to leave the meeting entirely. He feels an overwhelming urge to get out of the situation.

"I can't do this right now. I need to step outside," he says abruptly, standing up and heading for the door. Michael uses delay tactics to avoid making decisions, asking for more time and additional breaks. "Can we continue this discussion next week? I need to think about this more." Michael's flight response disrupts the negotiation process and his avoidance behavior prevents productive discussion and resolution of important issues, prolonging the overall process and increasing stress for both parties.

But Michael is embarrassed by his inability to act. This morning, he had a proposal that is pretty darn close to the option suggested by Laura's attorney but he is terrified about what he doesn't know. If Laura's attorney is suggesting the same idea, then he must be missing something. He wishes that he could say "I was thinking something pretty close to that, and I'm wondering if we could talk about the pros and cons for each of us."

Freeze Response

Sometimes, the body responds to anxiety by freezing, making a person feel paralyzed or unable to act. This response can be seen as a way to avoid detection and hope that the perceived aggressor loses interest. During the freeze response, there may be a drop in heart rate, a sense of numbness, or an inability to speak or move.

In divorce negotiations, this can make someone feel unable to even consider any movement at all. All options seem terrifying. Here's what it looks and sounds like:

Aurora and Pierre are in the midst of divorce negotiations. Aurora is particularly anxious about the spousal support terms, fearing that she will be left financially unstable. The stress of the situation is overwhelming to her.

During a negotiation meeting, Pierre's attorney presents a proposed spousal support agreement that Aurora finds shocking and overwhelming. Her anxiety triggers the freeze response. Aurora becomes physically still, sitting rigid in her chair with a blank expression on her face. Her hands are clasped tightly in her lap, and she stares at the documents without blinking or reacting.

Aurora struggles to articulate her thoughts or respond to questions. When asked for her opinion, she responds with a barely audible and shaky, "I don't know," or she remains completely silent. Aurora experiences difficulty thinking clearly and processing information. Her mind is foggy, and she cannot make decisions or consider alternatives. To cope with the overwhelming anxiety, Aurora seems to have detached emotionally, feeling numb and disconnected from the situation. She appears disengaged and unresponsive, as if she is not fully present in the room.

Aurora's freeze response stalls the negotiation process. Her inability to participate actively makes it difficult to address and resolve key issues, leading to frustration for both parties and the mediator, who has noticed that she is not following the conversation. Trying to get Aurora's response prolongs the negotiations, and her freezing could result in a settlement that does not fully address her needs and concerns.

Aurora, herself, is frustrated by her foggy head in these negotiations. She has good ideas at home, but her anxiety completely overwhelms her in the sessions and renders her unable to think anything through. She feels stupid and each session has her thinking she needs someone to do this for her even though she hates the idea of another person taking over negotiating what is going to happen with her life.

How Anxiety Undermines You

In all three of the scenarios—fight, flight, and freeze—anxiety makes you reactive and defensive, causing you to lose your emotional balance. When anxiety takes hold, your ability to think clearly and rationally diminishes, often leading to heightened emotional responses and making impulsive decisions. In this state, you may find yourself reacting to situations based on fear rather than carefully considering the best course of action. This defensiveness can manifest as aggression, avoidance, or withdrawal, all of which hinder productive communication and problem-solving during divorce negotiations.

When you are in a highly anxious place, it is hard to come to divorce negotiations or even think about how you might best approach them. The intense emotional strain of anxiety makes it difficult to focus on the details and complexities involved in the negotiation process. You might struggle to articulate your needs and concerns effectively, and important aspects of the settlement may be overlooked or miscommunicated. Anxiety can also impair your ability to listen to and understand the perspectives of others, which is crucial for finding a mutually agreeable solution.

Divorce is naturally anxiety-provoking. The end of a marriage represents a significant life change, filled with uncertainty about the future. Concerns about financial stability, living arrangements, and the well-being of any children involved can all contribute to a heightened state of anxiety. The adversarial nature of divorce proceedings, coupled with the emotional baggage of the relationship, further exacerbates this stress. As a result, navigating divorce negotiations often feels overwhelming and fraught with tension, making it challenging to approach the situation with a calm and clear mind.

Anxiety fundamentally alters your mental and emotional state, disconnecting you from your best self. This disconnection is characterized by several key factors that undermine your ability to function optimally and maintain a healthy perspective:

Anxiety can make you struggle to articulate your needs and concerns effectively, and important aspects of the settlement may be overlooked or miscommunicated.

- **Impaired decision-making:** Anxiety clouds your judgment, making it difficult to think clearly and make rational decisions. When anxious, you are more likely to react impulsively rather than consider all options thoughtfully. This can lead to choices that do not align with your values or long-term goals.

- **Emotional overwhelm:** High levels of anxiety can flood you with intense emotions such as fear, worry, and dread. These emotions can be all-consuming, making it hard to access the more balanced, calm, and rational parts of yourself. Emotional overwhelm often results in overreactions or emotional shutdowns, neither of which reflect your best self.

- **Reduced self-confidence:** Anxiety often brings with it a sense of self-doubt and inadequacy. It can make you question your abilities and decisions, eroding your self-esteem. This lack of confidence can prevent you from asserting your needs and standing up for yourself, which is essential during negotiations or challenging situations.

- **Physical symptoms:** Anxiety manifests physically, leading to symptoms like increased heart rate, sweating, trembling, and tension. These physical symptoms can be distracting and uncomfortable, further taking you away from a state of being calm and centered.

- **Narrowed focus:** When anxious, your focus tends to narrow in on the perceived threat or problem, often to the exclusion of other important aspects of life. This tunnel vision can prevent you from seeing the bigger picture and considering broader implications or alternative solutions.

- **Diminished coping skills:** Chronic anxiety can wear down your coping mechanisms, making it harder to handle stress in healthy ways. You might resort to avoidance, denial, or other maladaptive strategies that do not reflect your best self's resilience and problem-solving capabilities.

- **Interpersonal strain:** Anxiety can strain your relationships with others. It can cause you to misinterpret social cues, become overly defensive or withdrawn, and react in ways that push others away. This can lead to conflicts and misunderstandings that further isolate you and prevent you from accessing the support and connection that are part of your best self.

If you want to manage anxiety and remain grounded during divorce negotiations, it is important to develop strategies for self-regulation and emotional resilience. Techniques such as mindfulness, deep breathing, and grounding exercises can help you stay present and focused. Seeking support from a therapist, coach, or counselor can provide you with tools to cope with anxiety and work through the emotional aspects of divorce. Additionally, being well prepared and having a clear understanding of your goals and priorities can empower you to engage in negotiations more confidently and effectively. You can create a more constructive and less stressful environment for resolving the issues that come up during your divorce when you address anxiety proactively. And doing so can even help you uncover the deeper meaning behind your emotions.

Turning Anxiety Into Insight

One day I was talking with my wise friend Norman Fischer who served as co-abbot of the San Francisco Zen Center from 1995 to 2000, after which he founded the Everyday Zen Foundation in 2000. We were discussing anxiety and my personal struggles with it, and he shared a Buddhist saying that completely changed how I viewed anxiety and how it could help me.

> If you follow your afflictive emotions all the way to their roots, you will find a Buddha sitting on a lotus flower.

I was stunned. What if I didn't try to avoid my anxiety and work feverishly to find a way to make it go away as quickly as possible at almost any cost? What if I sat with it instead and figured out what was going on for me in a way that I may not yet know?

What if, instead of pushing anxiety away, you used it as a guide? Could it point you toward something deeper that you need to address? Could anxiety actually help you understand yourself better and lead you to a better place? Hard to believe, but it may actually be possible.

Experiencing anxiety is hard, but it is not something to feel bad about, nor is it something to try to avoid. It is your brain trying to help you, and while it can feel awful and, at its worst, you might feel like you are having a heart attack, it does have useful information for you. Anxiety, though often viewed as a negative and overwhelming emotion, can serve as a powerful teacher, especially in the context of a divorce. By exploring what your anxiety reveals, you can gain valuable insights and leverage this knowledge for personal growth and better decision-making.

So, what's in it for you? Well, here are some benefits of anxiety.

Self-Awareness

Anxiety often highlights areas of your life that need attention. It can bring to the surface unresolved issues, unmet needs, and deep-seated fears. By paying attention to what triggers your anxiety, you can gain a clearer understanding of what truly matters to you and where you need to focus your efforts for healing and growth.

For example, Emily noticed that she felt most anxious about financial stability. This self-awareness prompted her to take financial planning courses, consult a financial advisor, and create a budget. As a result, she gained confidence in her ability to manage her finances post-divorce.

Emotional Intelligence

Experiencing anxiety can enhance your emotional intelligence by helping you recognize and understand your emotions more deeply. This increased awareness allows you to manage your emotions more effectively, respond to others with greater empathy, and navigate complex interpersonal dynamics with more skill. It can also help you put recovery strategies in place for when anxiety occurs.

Leo realized that his anxiety was causing him to be overly defensive during negotiations with his ex. By acknowledging his anxiety and working on his emotional intelligence, he learned to communicate more calmly and empathetically. This improved their interactions and facilitated a more amicable settlement.

Resilience Building

Facing and working through anxiety builds resilience. Each time you confront your anxiety and find ways to cope, you strengthen your ability to handle future stressors. This resilience is particularly valuable during divorce, a period often marked by significant change and uncertainty. It also helps you build a new relationship with your ex if that is necessary because of children or a shared business or property.

Lisa faced severe anxiety about her ability to co-parent effectively. Through therapy and support groups, she developed coping strategies that made her more resilient. Over time, she became more confident in her parenting skills and better equipped to handle co-parenting challenges. Her relationship with her ex also improved over time as she became a more willing and available co-parenting partner.

NOW THAT you understand how useful anxiety can be, it's also helpful to explore what other feelings anxiety might be hiding because those feelings can give you more insight into yourself. I discussed some of these emotions in the previous chapter, but here are some of the more common issues I see:

- **Fear:** Anxiety often masks deeper fears, such as fear of the unknown, fear of financial instability, or fear of losing your relationship with your children. Recognizing these fears can help you address them directly and find ways to mitigate their impact.

- **Sadness and loss:** Underneath anxiety, there may be feelings of sadness and grief over the loss of your marriage and the life you

In relationships, anxiety often highlights concerns about connection, trust, and loyalty, helping you see what you value most in your interactions.

envisioned. Acknowledging and processing these feelings is crucial for healing and moving forward.

- **Anger and frustration:** Anxiety can also cover up anger and frustration, toward either your ex or the situation as a whole. Identifying these emotions allows you to deal with them constructively, rather than letting them fester and exacerbate your anxiety.

- **Guilt and shame:** Feelings of guilt or shame about or surrounding the divorce can manifest as anxiety. Understanding these underlying emotions can help you practice self-compassion and forgive yourself for any perceived failures or shortcomings.

When you experience anxiety, it often signals that something important to you is at stake. That means when you take the time to examine the sources and triggers of your anxiety, you can gain clarity on what truly matters to you and your core values.

Exploring Anxiety to Reveal Your Core Values

Anxiety often arises when something you deeply care about is threatened, so paying attention to its triggers can help you identify your true priorities. Sometimes anxiety signals a perceived injustice or conflict with personal values, indicating that your principles are being challenged. It can also stem from unmet needs tied to those core values, revealing what truly matters to you at a deeper level.

In relationships, anxiety often highlights concerns about connection, trust, and loyalty, helping you see what you value most in your interactions. By recognizing how anxiety pushes you to protect these values, you can take purposeful actions that reflect your deepest beliefs and priorities.

In her book *Emotional Agility*, Susan David provides a comprehensive framework for understanding and navigating emotions, including anxiety, to uncover and align with your core values. I've put together some tips using her insights and strategies to help you mine your anxiety for valuable information about your core values. Each of these tips incorporates a specific divorce example and an action that you might consider taking when you feel this response.

Reflect On Your Triggers

Emotions are data, not directives. Anxiety often arises in response to situations where our core values are threatened or unmet. For example, Alina noticed anxiety in herself when she was discussing custody arrangements, highlighting her core value of being a present and involved parent.

Action: Identify specific situations or thoughts that trigger your anxiety. Keep a journal to track these instances and note any patterns that emerge. Consider what values might be underlying these triggers.

Ask Reflective Questions

Use self-reflection to uncover deeper truths. Reflective questions can help you understand the root causes of your anxiety. Bob asked himself why meeting his ex's attorney caused anxiety and realized it was due to feeling unprepared, revealing his core value of competence.

Action: When you feel anxious, ask yourself questions like, What am I afraid of losing? or What principle do I feel is being violated? This will help you dig deeper and gain clarity on what matters most to you.

Explore Your Underlying Emotions

Embrace all emotions, including anxiety, to gain insight into your values. Emotions act as signals pointing to what is important. Stacy's anxiety about financial independence led her to realize that security and self-sufficiency were core values she held.

Action: Examine the emotions beneath your anxiety. Are you feeling fear, sadness, anger, or frustration? These emotions can provide clues about your core values.

Look for Patterns

Recognize recurring themes in your emotional responses. These patterns often point to your core values. Anton noticed a pattern of anxiety related to feeling disrespected, revealing his core value of mutual respect and dignity.

Action: Review your anxiety triggers and associated emotions to identify recurring themes. These themes often highlight your core values.

Seek Professional Guidance

Working with a therapist or coach can provide a structured environment to explore and understand your emotions and values. Karen's therapist helped her explore her anxiety about the future, uncovering her core value of stability and planning.

Action: Therapy offers a safe space for self-discovery. A therapist can help you delve into the roots of your anxiety and uncover hidden emotions and values.

Practice Mindfulness

Mindfulness allows you to observe your emotions without judgment, helping you understand their underlying causes. John used mindfulness meditation to stay grounded during stressful negotiation sessions, helping him realize his core value of inner peace.

Action: Engage in mindfulness practices to stay present and observe your anxiety. This can prevent you from becoming overwhelmed and allow you to gain insight into your emotional state. A 2011 study published in *Psychiatry Research: Neuroimaging*, led by Sara Lazar and colleagues at Massachusetts General, Harvard Medical School's teaching hospital, found that participants who completed an eight-week mindfulness-based stress reduction (MBSR) program exhibited increased gray matter density in the hippocampus, which is important for learning and memory, and in structures of the brain associated with self-awareness, compassion, and introspection.

Additionally, reductions in the size of the amygdala were observed, correlating with decreased stress levels.

Reframe Your Anxiety

View anxiety as useful information rather than a threat. Reframing anxiety as a signal helps you understand its significance. Rose started viewing her anxiety as a signal to address important issues, leading to proactive steps that aligned with her core values.

Action: Reframe your anxiety as a signal pointing to important values. This perspective can reduce the fear associated with anxiety and empower you to address its root causes.

Do Something

Aligning your actions with your values leads to greater authenticity and well-being. Liam's anxiety about financial security motivated him to take a financial planning course, aligning his actions with his core value of financial independence.

Action: Use the information gleaned from your anxiety to make informed decisions and take meaningful action. Whether it's setting boundaries, seeking financial advice, or prioritizing self-care, acting on this knowledge can help reduce anxiety and improve your overall well-being.

ANXIETY CAN be transformed from a source of distress into a tool for uncovering your core values. This approach not only helps you navigate the immediate stressors of divorce but also equips you with valuable tools for future challenges. Embracing and working through anxiety with curiosity and compassion can lead to profound personal growth and a deeper understanding of your true self. But that doesn't mean it will go away forever, so you need to be prepared for the eventuality of its return.

Practical Steps for Managing Returning Anxiety

Even after working to manage anxiety and uncover your core values, it's normal for anxiety to return, especially during stressful times like a divorce. When that happens, try returning to some of these strategies to help you reset and re-center:

- acknowledge and accept it
- engage in mindfulness practices
- identify the trigger
- revisit your core values
- use reflective questions
- engage in self-care
- seek support
- practice self-compassion
- reframe negative thoughts
- develop an action plan
- maintain a gratitude journal

Anxiety doesn't have to derail your divorce negotiations or take control of your life. By learning to sit with your anxiety, identify its roots, and use it to guide your decisions, you can make choices that align with your values and lead you toward a future that feels secure and fulfilling. Take a deep breath, lean into the discomfort, and trust that you have the strength to navigate this challenge.

Anxiety is an almost inevitable companion in divorce negotiations. But while anxiety often feels overwhelming, it carries a message worth listening to because it signals what truly matters to you. Ignoring or suppressing these feelings might seem like the easiest path, but doing so can lead to impulsive decisions, stalled discussions, or, worse, a resolution that does not address what is most important.

Instead, by leaning into your emotions, you can uncover insights that not only clarify your priorities but also strengthen your ability to communicate and negotiate effectively. In the next chapter, we'll explore how embracing emotions—even the difficult ones—can open the door to deeper understanding, greater empowerment, and better outcomes in your divorce process.

KEY TAKEAWAYS

- **Recognize anxiety as guidance:** View anxiety not as a barrier but as a signal highlighting unmet needs and deeper values.

- **Explore your core values:** When you feel anxious and explore the perceived threat or unmet need, you clarify what's most important to you—whether it's fairness, connection, trust, or security.

- **Understand your emotional triggers:** Acknowledge that anxiety may mask other emotions like fear, sadness, or guilt, offering insight into underlying concerns.

- **Move beyond reactive responses:** Shift from impulsive fight, flight, or freeze behaviors to thoughtful, values-driven actions.

- **Take proactive steps:** Channel your anxiety into decisive action by setting boundaries, seeking support, and actively shaping a secure future.

5

Lean Into Your Emotions

AFTER FIFTEEN YEARS of marriage, Amanda and Jason found themselves deep in divorce negotiations. They shared two teenage children and co-owned a family business. During the discussions, Amanda repeatedly pushed for full ownership of the family business; her insistence minimized Jason's role in creating the business, leaving Jason defensive and leading to an impasse and widespread frustration. To the mediator, it initially seemed like a classic financial dispute—until Amanda was encouraged to explore and express her emotions.

One sleepless night, Amanda turned to a journal her divorce coach had given her. Sitting with a cup of tea, she began to write, hoping to uncover what was truly driving her demands. Amanda realized that her determination wasn't just about finances; it was deeply tied to her fear of losing her sense of identity. For years, she had poured herself into managing the business while also raising their children. Surrendering the business felt like she was losing a core part of herself. This insight allowed her to articulate her feelings to Jason—not as a demand but as a need for acknowledgment and security.

In their next mediation session, Jason listened closely to Amanda as she shared her fears. Encouraged by her candor, he opened up too: his resistance to letting go of the business stemmed from a fear of financial instability and uncertainty about starting over alone. These revelations shifted the tone of their negotiations. They began working creatively, drawing on the collaborative strengths that had once made their business successful. Together, they agreed to transition the business into a shared asset for a defined period. Amanda would manage the daily operations, reflecting her dedication and expertise, while Jason would step back but retain a minority stake. This arrangement honored both Amanda's connection to the business and Jason's financial needs.

By leaning into their emotions—the guiding principle of this book—Amanda and Jason moved beyond a battle of positions to craft a solution that respected their shared history and individual futures. When we recognize how our deepest fears, hopes, and unmet needs color every interaction, we can move beyond mere positional bargaining into authentic communication. At the same time, we create an opening for genuine progress in divorce negotiations and beyond.

Turning Emotions Into Insight

I have a cherished friend who's unafraid to ask hard questions and deliver uncomfortable truths. Though I value all my friends' support, I especially treasure this one because she doesn't just aim to make me feel better, she helps me understand what I'm feeling and why. Her honesty transforms emotional reactions into insights I can act on—a clarity that is invaluable in life's most challenging moments—and a lesson that has been crucial throughout my career.

As a young litigator, I quickly learned that the courtroom is a bad place to discover the other side has a good point. Understanding all sides of a story—including my own emotions and biases—is essential. It doesn't make you weaker to understand where the other side is coming from; in fact it makes you much stronger. Divorce negotiations often mirror courtroom battles, with each party entrenched in "right" versus "wrong." But this black-and-white thinking oversimplifies complex situations, leaving little room for meaningful resolution in negotiation. Emotions shape each person's perspective, making their stance feel justified and indisputable.

Early in my marriage, I faced this dynamic when I asked my husband about his plans for a busy weekend. His sharp "what do you want?" response always stung. I thought I was asking an innocent question, but his reaction felt accusatory. It took years for me to realize I did want something: I wanted help managing a packed weekend schedule. Over time I learned to say, "It's going to be a busy weekend. Let's figure out how to get the kids where they need to be while also making time for ourselves."

This shift—understanding my own emotions and communicating them clearly—transformed tension into collaboration. The same principle applies in divorce negotiation. Emotions often drive a person's position, even when they are unaware of this. Amanda and Jason's apparent financial disagreement, for instance, was rooted in deeper fears and insecurities. By exploring these emotions, they reframed their conflict and moved from opposition to cooperation.

Understanding your emotions is foundational to effective problem-solving. It allows you to step out of the "right versus wrong" mindset and see the bigger picture. When you can identify what you're feeling and why, you're better equipped to articulate your needs, understand others' perspectives, and find creative, lasting solutions to even the most difficult conflicts.

In chapter 3, I introduced an exercise and showed you how Marcy used it to navigate her emotions and her priorities. By writing down her thoughts with compassion—for herself and her ex, Steve—Marcy moved from feeling like a victim to becoming a proactive problem-solver. Through curiosity-driven exploration, Marcy not only identified her own needs but also considered Steve's perspective. This clarity helped her approach their divorce negotiations with empathy and purpose.

When Marcy felt overwhelmed, she paused and asked herself why. She leaned on a trusted friend to help her breathe through the moments of pain and anxiety, completing the exercise despite her discomfort. This process of curiosity and reflection turned emotional chaos into insights. And those insights led to productive conversations between her and Steve and, ultimately, to meaningful solutions.

But although Marcy was able to show herself compassion when she noticed anger toward Steve was rising, that kind of self-compassion is not always easy to achieve.

Be Kind to Yourself

Divorce is a profoundly painful experience that often stirs a deep sense of vulnerability and shame. The language commonly used to describe divorce amplifies these emotions—phrases like "failed marriage" or "broken family" carry heavy implications of personal failure and inadequacy. This stigma reinforces feelings of isolation and unworthiness, making an already difficult process feel overwhelming. Even hearing the word "shame" can evoke a visceral reaction.

For instance, Archie—a client who prided himself on always doing "the right thing"—felt immense shame simply because his divorce conflicted with his own deeply held beliefs about marriage. As a culture, we are ill-equipped to handle shame. It's a complex and deeply ingrained emotion that thrives in secrecy and silence.

Brené Brown has written extensively about the powerful and challenging emotions of shame and vulnerability, and her insights have profoundly changed how we think and talk about these feelings. One of her key findings is that shame thrives in secrecy and silence, but it begins to lose its grip when we name it and meet it with empathy. Brown defines shame resilience as the ability to recognize shame, move through it with awareness and self-compassion, and connect with others to restore a sense of worthiness.

Dr. Brown's work offers hope: By naming and confronting our shame, we begin to dismantle its grip. Shame resilience involves understanding our personal triggers, reframing the internal narratives we tell ourselves, and cultivating empathy—both for ourselves and from trusted others. This process allows us to transform vulnerability from something to fear into a gateway to authenticity and strength. One powerful takeaway from Dr. Brown's research is that vulnerability—the very thing we often avoid—is essential for personal growth and authenticity. By facing our shame head-on, we can live fuller, more meaningful lives. For those navigating divorce, this message is particularly relevant. Vulnerability opens the door to self-compassion, clarity, and renewal.

American cultural anthropologist Margaret Mead exemplified this perspective beautifully. When asked why her marriages "failed," she replied, "I have been married three times, and not one of them was a failure." Her response highlights the possibility of accepting relationships for everything they were, including their endings. Mead's outlook reminds us that divorce does not erase the love or value that existed within a marriage; rather, it marks an evolution. This shift in mindset allows us to honor the relationship and gives us the courage it takes to let go.

Learning to be kind to yourself, especially when shame and vulnerability feel overwhelming is just one step. You also need practical tools like resilience, hope, and planning that help you turn self-compassion into forward momentum.

Building Resilience and Hope

Divorce may signify the end of something familiar, but it also marks the beginning of something new—something often filled with uncertainty. The unknown can be daunting, but it also holds the potential for transformation. Resilience, hope, and planning are three tools that can help navigate this journey:

- **Resilience** is often misunderstood. It's not about toughing it out or pretending everything's fine. In American culture, especially for men, resilience is frequently confused with emotional suppression: the idea that "when the going gets tough, the tough get going." But true resilience is about flexibility, self-compassion, and the willingness to feel your emotions and still move forward. It means facing adversity honestly, asking for help when needed, and adapting through the experience. In the context of divorce, resilience allows you to navigate the highs and lows with clarity and confidence, discovering strength you may not have known you had.

- **Hope** gives us a vision for the future. It keeps us moving forward, reminding us that life beyond divorce can be fulfilling and joyful.
- **Planning** provides the road map. By setting clear goals and taking actionable steps, we can transform uncertainty into a sense of control and direction.

When we combine resilience, hope, and planning, we can reframe divorce as an opportunity for reinvention. This doesn't mean the pain of divorce disappears, but it does mean we can approach the future with purpose and possibility. By fostering these qualities, divorce becomes not just an end, but also a powerful beginning. Margaret Mead's ability to embrace both the successes and endings of her marriages shows how self-compassion allows us to move forward without self-judgment. Like Mead, we can see divorce as part of a larger story of growth, not failure.

Cultivating resilience and hope can guide us through the uncertainties of divorce, but even with the best intentions, we may still find ourselves locked in old patterns. Sometimes, our desire to be "right" overshadows our longing for peace. How do we break free?

Do You Want to Be Happy or Right?

In the prologue to her book *The Dance of Connection*, Harriet Lerner, PhD, shares a story about parents watching two children playing in a sandbox. A fight erupts, and one child storms off, shouting, "I hate you! I hate you!" But moments later, the children are back in the sandbox, playing together as if nothing had happened. Observing this, one parent asked, "How do children do that? They were enemies five minutes ago." The other parent replied, "It's simple. They choose happiness over righteousness."

When you are navigating the betrayal and anger often tied to divorce, choosing happiness over righteousness can feel far more complicated. Divorce can intensify the belief that one's perspective is the "right" one and that the other person is fundamentally wrong. Years of feeling misunderstood or undervalued can lead to a downward spiral of frustration and defensiveness. The challenge, then, is how to move beyond these patterns to communicate effectively about the things that matter most.

Sharon and Rhys' story highlights the difficulty of finding a shared understanding amid the emotional turbulence of divorce. Married for many years, with two adult children, Sharon was the primary breadwinner while Rhys was a musician who freelanced. Their marriage ended after Sharon discovered that Rhys had had an affair—his second. Understandably hurt and angry, Sharon wanted to finalize their divorce as quickly as possible, while Rhys' remorse made him eager to cooperate.

Despite the emotional intensity of their situation, Sharon and Rhys managed to negotiate their divorce fairly and efficiently. When they came together to finalize their agreement, I told them how impressed I was by the dignity they showed during mediation, during such a challenging moment. Sharon burst into tears. "I thought we treated each other terribly," she said. Even through her anger, Sharon had found a way to prioritize a sense of fairness and her long-term goals for their family. Over time, she consciously chose to focus on what mattered most—her relationship with her children and a future where she and Rhys could coexist peacefully. This choice helped her see Rhys not through the lens of betrayal but as someone she could continue to work with for the good of their family.

Conflict often traps us in predictable and unproductive cycles, and divorce can magnify these patterns. One key to breaking the cycle is to focus on what truly matters and to speak from a place of authenticity, rather than defensiveness or blame. This is no small task, especially when emotions are raw. However, it is possible to communicate in a way that prioritizes clarity, connection, and the person you want to be—even if your ex doesn't reciprocate.

In her book *The Good Karma Divorce*, Judge Michele Lowrance encourages individuals to define the kind of person they want to be throughout the divorce process—a guiding principle that can serve as an emotional anchor during times of conflict. This idea is echoed in the work of psychologist Dr. Harriet Lerner, who writes in *The Dance of Connection*, "The challenge in conversation is not just to be ourselves, but to choose the self we want to be." Sharon, for instance, found clarity by reconnecting with her priorities and values. She wanted to be someone her children could admire, and this perspective helped her shift from anger to authenticity.

Reframing the "Conflict" Between Right and Happy

Choosing happiness doesn't mean suppressing your feelings or ignoring the wrongs you've experienced. Instead, it's about intentionally creating the future you want for yourself and your family. This requires support—whether from a therapist, coach, or trusted friend—to help you articulate your needs and maintain focus on your goals. When you approach the process with self-awareness and intention, you not only make better decisions but also emerge with a sense of dignity and peace.

Your internal world—not external circumstances—determines much of your happiness. This truth is especially relevant during divorce. I've seen clients in nearly identical circumstances emerge with completely different outlooks and outcomes. One may remain mired in resentment, while the other focuses on building a brighter future. The difference often lies in the ability to reframe the experience and cultivate resilience.

For instance, Theo felt deeply wronged during his divorce, but rather than dwelling on his anger, he worked with a therapist to identify what he truly wanted: stability for his children and a fresh start

Conflict often traps us in predictable and unproductive cycles, and divorce can magnify these patterns.

for himself. By focusing on these goals, Theo found the motivation to take constructive actions, like creating a supportive routine for his kids and finding a new home. Eventually, he remarried, and he told me that the lessons he learned during his divorce helped him build a stronger, healthier second marriage.

Divorce can be an opportunity for profound growth and transformation if approached with intentionality and an open heart. Here are some practical steps to help you reframe the conflict between being "right" and creating happiness:

- **Define your priorities:** Ask yourself who you want to be during and after the divorce. What legacy do you want to leave for your children or yourself?

- **Focus on positivity:** Identify what you want to achieve rather than fixating on what you've lost or what you feel entitled to. (It might be necessary to mourn what is lost before shifting your focus to positivity.)

- **Express gratitude:** Keeping a gratitude journal can help you focus on the good in your life and shift your perspective.

- **Seek support:** Find someone, whether a professional or a trusted confidant, who can help you process your emotions constructively.

- **Pause before reacting:** When conflict arises, rather than falling into old patterns, take a moment to reflect on what you truly want to communicate.

Finding Peace and Moving Forward

Divorce isn't just a legal or financial process—it's an emotional upheaval that requires deliberate effort to maintain a positive outlook. Gratitude can be a powerful tool. Sylvia, for example, found it difficult to stay positive during heated negotiations. Her therapist suggested keeping a gratitude journal to focus on the good in her life: supportive friends, her children's laughter, and her own resilience. This practice helped her approach negotiations with a calmer, more constructive mindset.

As you process the emotions surrounding your divorce, try to acknowledge the positives that came from your marriage. Instead of focusing solely on the ending, consider saying both "let go" and "thank you." Thank you for the children, for the shared joys, for the growth you experienced. This mindset doesn't minimize the pain but allows you to move forward with a sense of peace. Kristina chose to write a thank-you letter to her ex. She acknowledged the love and good times they shared, while also expressing her hope for healing and mutual respect. This act of gratitude wasn't about reconciling; it was about reclaiming her narrative and focusing on the positives.

Divorce often involves betrayal, hurt, and anger. Letting go of resentment, however, is essential for healing. As I've heard it put, "Holding on to resentment and anger is like eating rat poison and hoping the rat will die." Forgiveness doesn't mean excusing bad behavior or reconciling. It means freeing yourself from the emotional weight of the past. Dr. Janis Abrahms Spring offers two pathways for this: acceptance and genuine forgiveness. Acceptance involves acknowledging your pain and finding ways to release it without needing the other person's apology or remorse. Genuine forgiveness, on the other hand, requires accountability and amends from the person who hurt you, which isn't always possible. Making peace with your ex doesn't mean "letting them off the hook." It's about reclaiming your power and choosing to live your life free from the grip of resentment.

Ellen and Douglas, for example, faced this challenge after Douglas discovered Ellen's affair. With the help of a child specialist, they worked together to develop a script for telling their children about the divorce. Douglas's initial impulse to publicly blame Ellen shifted as he realized that protecting their children's emotional well-being was more important than assigning blame. Creating a shared narrative allowed them to move forward with dignity.

Letting go of anger isn't about absolving your ex—it's about setting yourself free so you can find peace and move on. Holding on to resentment means shaping your life around someone who hurt you. True freedom comes from releasing that anger and focusing on building the life you want for yourself and your children.

Acceptance Is the Key to Change

The *paradoxical theory of change*, rooted in Gestalt therapy and developed by Arnold Beisser, reveals a profound truth: genuine transformation begins with acceptance. Rather than rejecting or suppressing parts of ourselves, real progress comes from embracing who we are with self-awareness and validation. The harder we push to force change, the more resistance we encounter. By fully acknowledging and accepting our current state, we create space for natural growth to occur.

This principle applies to negotiation as well. People often resist change when they feel misunderstood or invalidated. In divorce discussions, individuals typically won't soften their stance or explore alternatives until they sense that they have been seen, heard, and affirmed. When their perspective is acknowledged—without judgment or dismissal—they become more receptive to creative solutions and meaningful collaboration. This means progress isn't driven by pressure or force. Instead, real change emerges when each party's emotions and underlying needs are acknowledged. By fostering understanding and validation, divorce negotiations can shift from a standoff over positions to a collaborative process that honors everyone's priorities.

Consider the mediation between Amanda and Jason, previously discussed. Amanda insisted on full ownership of the family business, leaving Jason feeling defensive and unacknowledged for his contributions. The turning point came when Jason reflected back Amanda's feelings: that the business was a core part of her identity and one she feared losing through the divorce. Feeling understood, Amanda became less defensive and more open to viewing the business as a shared asset rather than something she alone must claim. Likewise, when Amanda validated Jason's fears about financial instability, he became more willing to explore creative solutions that addressed both of their concerns.

Demonstrating understanding and validation has a powerful effect on the other person's behavior and attitudes in negotiation. When individuals feel heard, they tend to become less defensive and more willing to engage in genuine dialogue. For instance, acknowledging an ex-spouse's emotional attachment to a particular asset can encourage them to explore alternate solutions instead of digging in their heels. At the same time, recognizing someone's concerns fosters increased flexibility, because feeling understood opens the door to new perspectives and creative options. If you show empathy for your ex's worries about child custody, for example, it may prompt them to consider arrangements that benefit both parties, such as shared parenting.

Beyond reducing defensiveness and broadening flexibility, empathy also enhances cooperation. When you acknowledge an ex's financial anxieties or deeper fears, you signal a willingness to take their experiences seriously, which often leads them to respond in kind by striving for balanced solutions. This cycle of mutual understanding helps build trust and promotes a sense of goodwill on both sides. In turn, that trust and goodwill set the stage for a more balanced negotiation, since modeling understanding and acceptance naturally encourages the other person to do the same. Ultimately, an atmosphere of respect and empathy paves the way for constructive dialogue and meaningful outcomes that honor everyone's needs.

To apply the paradoxical theory of change in your own negotiations, consider these practical steps:

- **Engage in active listening:** Reflect back what you hear to show that you understand their perspective. For example, "I hear that you're very concerned about maintaining a stable environment for the children. That's really important." More on active listening in the next chapter.

- **Validate emotions:** Acknowledge their feelings without judgment. "It seems like you're feeling anxious about the financial uncertainty. That's completely understandable."

- **Express understanding:** Demonstrate that you're genuinely considering their viewpoint. "I see why you want to keep the house—it holds a lot of memories and feels like a place of security."

- **Ask open-ended questions:** Encourage them to share more about their concerns and priorities. "Can you help me understand what feels most important to you in this situation?"

- **Avoid immediate counterarguments:** Instead of arguing your point right away, take time to fully explore their perspective. "I get that you're worried about this arrangement. What do you think might work better for both of us?"

By fostering this kind of dialogue, you create an environment where change can emerge naturally. This approach doesn't just pave the way for creative solutions; it also allows both parties to leave the negotiation feeling understood and respected—a key element in achieving a resolution that truly works for everyone.

ULTIMATELY, "leaning into your emotions" is about accepting the full breadth of your internal experience—fears, frustrations, and vulnerabilities—as a source of information and insight. By allowing ourselves to explore and articulate these feelings, we can transform seemingly insurmountable conflicts into opportunities for collaboration and growth. From Amanda and Jason's experience, to embracing shame resilience, to applying the paradoxical theory of change, the common thread is the power of emotional honesty. When we grant ourselves permission to feel, we open the door to clarity and compassion—for ourselves and for those with whom we negotiate.

IN PART TWO of the book, I'm going to show you how to negotiate with and through your emotions. Our first stop in the next chapter will be to explore effective communication tactics that will empower you to navigate difficult conversations with clarity and confidence. These strategies are designed to help you articulate your needs, understand the other party's perspective, and create a collaborative atmosphere.

KEY TAKEAWAYS

- **Emotions are the foundation of negotiation:** In divorce negotiations, emotions often drive people's positions. Exploring both your and your ex's emotions can reveal the underlying needs and priorities that lead to productive solutions.

- **Shame and vulnerability are natural but manageable:** Divorce often brings feelings of shame and vulnerability. Developing resilience through self-compassion, acknowledging your emotions, and seeking support allows you to move forward with confidence.

- **Letting go of righteousness:** Eschewing the need to "win" or be "right" can create space for solutions that honor what truly matters to you and allow you to let go of resentment.

- **Acceptance is the key to genuine transformation:** Active listening, gratitude journaling, and engaging in therapy can help you embrace who you are and maintain a positive outlook.

PART TWO

NEGOTIATING WITH EMOTIONS

6

Elevating the Conversation

SEVERAL YEARS AGO, I gave a presentation to the Queens County Bar Association where I met a sitting judge. A few days later he invited me to lunch, asking me to meet him in his courtroom and wait until he finished his morning session. As I sat in the back of the courtroom, I observed the final minutes of his morning case, which was a divorce proceeding. The parties and their attorneys were lined up at the counsel table, facing the judge.

On the far left sat the husband, next to his lawyer. Beside them were the wife's two lawyers, and finally, on the far right sat the wife herself. They had reached a settlement and were putting it on the record. From the tension in the room, it was evident that this had been a contentious case, with every detail hotly debated.

At one point, the proceedings paused, and the judge asked, "Who is going to pay to repair the roof of the house?" Without hesitation, the husband stood up, looked over the heads of the row of attorneys, and spoke directly to his wife: "I'll pay for the roof," he said.

In that moment, the tone in the room shifted from competition and argument to one of agreement and cooperation. Once the tone changed, the husband became more generous, willing to take on a responsibility he might have resisted earlier. This example illustrates how a shift in tone can foster an atmosphere of agreement and collaboration, even in a contentious negotiation.

However, maintaining the right tone isn't always easy, especially when emotions run high. To help you navigate these challenges, let's explore some practical techniques for fostering a tone that encourages understanding and cooperation.

Powerful Non-Defensive Communication

One of the most effective strategies for maintaining the right tone in negotiations is through Powerful Non-Defensive Communication (PNDC). This approach, developed by Sharon Strand Ellison, focuses on expressing your needs and concerns without provoking defensiveness or escalating conflict. Communication experts widely agree that nonverbal cues—such as tone of voice, body language, and facial expressions—play a critical role in how messages are received. PNDC incorporates these elements to ensure that your words and nonverbal signals work together to foster understanding and cooperation.

Here's how to apply PNDC in your negotiations:

1. **Ask open-ended questions:** When inquiring about your ex's priorities, use open-ended questions that invite them to share their thoughts freely. For example, instead of asking "Why do you want the house?" try "What's most important to you when it comes to our property division?" This type of question is less likely to be perceived as confrontational and more likely to elicit meaningful, constructive responses.

2. **Use "I" statements:** Frame your concerns and needs using "I" statements rather than "you" statements. For instance, say "I'm concerned about how we'll manage parenting time" instead of "You never consider my schedule." This subtle shift focuses on your own experience rather than placing blame, reducing the likelihood of a defensive reaction. (I'll explore "I" statements in more detail later in the chapter, including how to structure them for maximum impact.)

3 **Acknowledge the other's perspective:** Demonstrate that you understand and respect your ex's perspective by acknowledging their concerns. For example, you might say "I understand that you want to ensure financial stability" before sharing your own priorities. This validation lowers emotional barriers and sets the stage for more productive discussions.

4 **Maintain a calm and steady tone:** Even when the conversation becomes difficult, strive to maintain calm. A steady tone keeps the discussion focused and constructive, even when emotions run high. In her book *Taking the War Out of Our Words*, Ellison highlights the importance of tone, specifically the inflection of your voice. She emphasizes that your inflection should go down, not up, at the end of each sentence. An upward inflection can unintentionally convey uncertainty or defensiveness, whereas a downward inflection projects confidence and clarity.

5 **Pay attention to nonverbal cues:** Nonverbal communication is just as important as what you say. Crossed arms or a raised voice can unintentionally signal defensiveness or aggression, even if your words are neutral. In contrast, maintaining open body language—such as uncrossed arms, relaxed posture, and steady eye contact—reinforces your verbal message and creates a sense of openness and collaboration. Aligning your nonverbal cues with a calm tone and confident delivery ensures that your message is received as intended.

By combining verbal strategies like open-ended questions with thoughtful attention to your nonverbal communication, you create an environment of trust and cooperation. These elements, working together, can transform even the most contentious conversations into opportunities for understanding and progress.

Reflective Listening

Reflective listening, an active listening skill often referred to as "looping," is a powerful tool for ensuring that communication during the divorce negotiation process remains clear and productive. This technique clarifies the other person's words and fosters understanding and respect, significantly enhancing the negotiation process. Beyond fostering connection, reflective listening offers several strategic benefits that can provide you with an advantage in negotiations.

So, what is reflective listening? At its core, reflective listening involves paraphrasing or summarizing the other person's words to confirm your understanding. This practice ensures that both parties are on the same page and that misunderstandings about what has been communicated are minimized. Additionally, reflective listening demonstrates genuine interest in and respect for the other person's perspective.

It's important to remember that understanding the other person's perspective—and telling them that you understand—does not mean agreeing with them. In fact, demonstrating that you understand their perspective without trying to change their mind is more likely to encourage them to align their perspective with yours than arguing ever could. Consider this: When was the last time you won an argument by convincing someone they were wrong?

Here are four reasons *why* reflective listening will aid you in your divorce negotiations:

1. **Clarifies communication:** Divorce negotiations often involve complex and sensitive issues, where misunderstandings can easily arise. Reflective listening helps clarify what the other person is saying, ensuring that you fully understand their concerns, priorities, and interests. By restating their points in your own words and checking for accuracy, you can prevent miscommunication and keep the conversation on track.

2. **Builds empathy and trust:** Reflective listening is an effective way to show empathy and build trust. When you take the time to accurately reflect what your ex has said, it signals that you are

listening carefully and that you value their perspective. This can reduce defensiveness and create a more cooperative atmosphere, making it easier to reach mutually beneficial agreements.

3. **De-escalates tension:** In heated discussions, emotions can quickly escalate, leading to conflict and communication breakdowns. Reflective listening can help reduce tension by slowing down the conversation and focusing on understanding rather than reacting. When the other person feels heard and understood, they are less likely to become defensive or combative, paving the way for more constructive dialogue.

4. **Ensures mutual understanding:** By looping back what the other person has said, you ensure that both parties have a mutual understanding of the issues being discussed. This is particularly important when making decisions or agreements, as it reduces the risk of later disputes over what was said or agreed upon.

How Reflective Listening Works

When you are actively listening and reflecting on what another person is saying you gain a deeper understanding of that person's priorities, concerns, and potential strategies. This insight allows you to adjust your approach and prepare more effective counteroffers. Also, when you accurately reflect the other person's points, they may feel encouraged to share more, revealing critical information that you can use strategically.

Here are several active ways reflective listening works in a negotiation situation:

1. **It controls the pace of negotiation:** Reflective listening naturally slows down the pace of conversation by creating pauses as you paraphrase and summarize. These pauses provide you with valuable time to think, plan, and formulate your next move. This can be particularly advantageous when the other party is pressuring you for quick decisions or when you need a moment to regain composure.

Reflective listening, or "looping," is a powerful tool for ensuring that communication during the divorce negotiation process remains clear and productive.

2 **It shifts the power dynamic:** By demonstrating understanding, you invite the other party to lower their guard and become more receptive to your perspective, subtly shifting the power dynamic. Additionally, when you show a willingness to listen, the other party is often more inclined to listen to you in return, creating a more balanced and cooperative negotiation environment.

3 **It fosters reciprocity:** Reflective listening fosters a sense of reciprocity in the negotiation. When you show that you're genuinely interested in understanding the other party's concerns, they are more likely to reciprocate and become open to your proposals. This dynamic can pave the way for a more collaborative and mutually beneficial outcome.

4 **It reduces resistance to proposals:** Validating the other party's concerns before presenting your own proposals reduces their resistance. When people feel heard and understood, they are more likely to consider alternative perspectives and solutions. This not only facilitates smoother negotiations but also allows you to weave their concerns into the narrative of your proposals, increasing the likelihood of acceptance.

These benefits aren't just anecdotal—they're backed by neuroscience research. Reflective listening activates the prefrontal cortex, the part of the brain responsible for empathy, reasoning, and emotional regulation. By engaging this region, you reduce the likelihood of reacting from the amygdala—the brain's threat center—which often leads to defensive or impulsive behavior. For a deeper dive into the science behind how intentional attention shapes the brain and improves emotional regulation, I recommend *Mindsight* by Dr. Daniel Siegel. This book offers a compelling explanation of how reflective practices like listening can literally rewire the brain to respond more effectively under stress.

Evie and Ezra: Creating Space for Problem-Solving

During one negotiation, I represented Evie who was seeking child support and alimony from her husband, Ezra, after their separation.

The couple had young twins, and Evie was concerned about ensuring financial stability for herself and their children. Ezra, however, was deeply resistant to the idea of long-term support payments.

Ezra had always dreamed of leaving corporate America to pursue a career as an author. For him, the financial obligations tied to the divorce felt like an insurmountable barrier to achieving that dream. As the negotiations progressed, it became clear that Ezra wasn't just talking about numbers; he was grieving the potential loss of a future he'd envisioned for himself.

In the middle of the discussion, I realized that Ezra needed to feel heard before he could engage in productive problem-solving. I decided to use reflective listening. I looped back to him what I'd heard him express: "Ezra, it sounds like this divorce is not just about the financial impact—it's about the loss of a dream you've had for a long time. It seems like stepping away from corporate life to focus on your writing is something that's deeply important to you, and this divorce feels like it's taking your ability to do that away." Then I paused...

When I acknowledged his pain, something shifted. For the first time in the negotiation, Ezra stopped repeating his frustrations about what he was giving up. Instead, he began to think aloud about how he might adjust his plans to balance both responsibilities—supporting his family and pursuing his writing aspirations. While it wasn't the future he had initially envisioned, Ezra was able to start considering a path forward that worked for everyone.

Just as reflective listening helped Ezra feel understood and enabled him to shift from frustration to problem-solving, you too can use this technique to create space for clarity, empathy, and constructive dialogue in your own negotiations.

Here's how to do that.

1 **Listen actively:** Focus fully on what the other person is saying without interrupting. Pay close attention to their words, tone, and body language to fully grasp their message. Resist the urge to mentally prepare your response while they are still speaking; instead, stay present in the moment.

2. **Paraphrase their message:** Once they've finished speaking, paraphrase their main points in your own words to confirm understanding. For example: "It seems like you're concerned about how we'll divide our time with the children and want to make sure their routines aren't disrupted. Is that correct?" This step demonstrates that you are actively listening and helps clarify their priorities.

3. **Check for understanding:** After paraphrasing, ask for confirmation to ensure you've accurately understood their perspective. A simple question like, "Did I get that right?" or "Is there anything I missed?" gives them an opportunity to clarify or expand on their points. If you skip this step, you risk making things worse by inadvertently substituting your version of their message for theirs, leaving them feeling even more unheard.

4. **Acknowledge their feelings:** Reflect not just the content of their words but also the emotions behind them. If they express frustration or concern, acknowledge those feelings by saying something like "It seems like this situation is really frustrating for you" or "I can understand why you're worried about that." This helps validate their emotions without necessarily agreeing with their position.

REFLECTIVE LISTENING doesn't mean you agree with the other person's position; it's about clarifying understanding and creating a space for constructive dialogue. It's normal to find this technique difficult, especially when you strongly disagree. However, when you view it as a way to gather accurate information and demonstrate that you're hearing the other person, reflective listening can ease tension and lead to better conversations—all without compromising your stance.

Although reflective listening is a vital tool for fostering understanding and reducing conflict in negotiations, when you combine it with tactical empathy you add a strategic dimension to your interactions. Tactical empathy uses that understanding you've gained in your reflective listening to influence the negotiation and guide the conversation toward mutually beneficial outcomes.

Tactical Empathy

As Chris Voss emphasizes in *Never Split the Difference*, *tactical empathy* is the ability to recognize and articulate the other party's emotions—and then use that insight strategically. By aligning with their feelings and concerns, you can build trust, gather valuable information, and encourage collaboration.

Tactical empathy demonstrates that you value the other party's perspective, which lowers defenses and fosters trust. This trust provides a foundation for open, constructive dialogue, making contentious issues easier to navigate.

In emotionally charged negotiations such as divorce, people often withhold what matters most. Tactical empathy encourages them to share crucial information—sometimes unintentionally. By acknowledging their emotions and concerns, you create a safe environment for them to open up, revealing hidden priorities and fears that guide the negotiation.

Tactical empathy lets you steer the conversation without provoking resistance. When people feel understood, they are more likely to engage cooperatively, take your proposals seriously, and reciprocate empathy.

When emotions run high, validating the other party's feelings can defuse tension and foster a more constructive atmosphere. Acknowledging their concerns does not imply agreement; it shows respect for their emotions, which reduces defensiveness and encourages openness. This approach also counters *reactive devaluation*—the tendency to dismiss proposals simply because they come from a perceived adversary. By demonstrating empathy, you allow your ex to judge your ideas on merit rather than rejecting them reflexively.

Fostering collaboration begins with recognizing and addressing the other party's emotions. Tactical empathy transforms a win-lose standoff into a joint effort to solve problems. By creating a sense of partnership, you pave the way for solutions that address both sides' needs, leading to more mutually beneficial outcomes.

Tactical Empathy in Negotiations

Using tactical empathy strengthens your position in negotiations. By demonstrating genuine investment in finding solutions—rather than pushing your own agenda—you enhance credibility and build trust. This approach encourages the other party to see you as reasonable and collaborative, making them more open to compromise and increasing the likelihood of favorable results.

Power imbalances are common in divorce negotiations, whether due to financial disparities, differences in assertiveness, or varying levels of negotiation experience. Tactical empathy can act as a powerful equalizer. When you show genuine understanding of the other person's needs and concerns, you can encourage them to lower their defenses and promote a more cooperative atmosphere. This supports constructive dialogue and helps both parties feel the process is fair, even when their negotiating strengths differ.

For instance, if one person dominates the conversation through sheer assertiveness, tactical empathy can subtly shift the power dynamic. By actively listening and validating their emotions, you can disarm their drive to control, leading to more balanced discussions. Similarly, if one party holds most of the financial power, tactical empathy can refocus the negotiation on shared interests, emphasizing collaboration over competition. This helps make the process more manageable and productive, regardless of initial power disparities.

If you're navigating a high-conflict divorce, showing empathy might feel like excusing your ex's behavior or letting them off the hook. It's understandable to resist this, especially if you see them as the primary source of your problems. However, tactical empathy isn't about condoning bad behavior; it's about using your understanding as a strategic tool to reach a more constructive and favorable outcome.

Consider this: the FBI developed tactical empathy to negotiate with some of the world's most dangerous individuals in highly charged situations. If it works in those high-stakes circumstances, it can certainly work in your divorce negotiations. Acknowledging the other person's emotions doesn't mean endorsing their actions; it simply creates a path beyond rigid positions, fostering a more cooperative stance that ultimately benefits you. Viewing empathy through this strategic lens can make it easier to adopt, even when doing so feels challenging.

Reflective listening and tactical empathy are invaluable tools for understanding the other person's perspective and fostering collaboration. Equally important is your ability to express your own thoughts and feelings in a way that encourages dialogue rather than conflict. This is where those "I" statements I mentioned earlier in the chapter come into play.

Using "I" Statements to Communicate Effectively

"I" statements let you share your concerns constructively and minimize defensiveness by focusing on your own experience rather than assigning blame. In emotionally charged discussions, it's easy to point fingers, which often escalates conflict. By contrast, "I" statements provide a constructive alternative, enabling you to express your needs and feelings without getting the other person's back up.

Instead of emphasizing what the other person is doing wrong, "I" statements center on your perspective, making it easier for the other person to hear and understand your concerns. For example, rather than saying "You never respect my time," you might say "I feel frustrated when plans change at the last minute because it disrupts my schedule."

"I" statements also shift the tone from confrontation to collaboration. When you frame concerns around your own experiences, the other party is less likely to feel attacked, which helps reduce defensiveness and keeps dialogue open. By clearly stating your feelings and needs, you lower the risk of misunderstandings and encourage the other party to focus on finding solutions rather than reacting negatively. Over time, this approach can foster a more cooperative atmosphere, even in the most emotionally charged discussions.

A Note on "I" Statements

"I" statements are often recommended because they help reduce defensiveness and shift the conversation away from blame. In theory, they allow you to express your experience without triggering the other person's amygdala—the brain's threat detector. But here's the catch: not all "I" statements are created equal.

Starting a sentence with "I" doesn't automatically make it non-blaming. I've worked with plenty of clients (and, let's be honest, I've done this myself) who say things like, "I just get upset because you always do that, and I don't like it." Technically, it starts with "I," but it's still a blame delivery system. The real power of "I" statements comes from owning your feelings and linking them to your values—not your ex's perceived failings.

Used thoughtfully, an "I" statement can short-circuit reactivity and open space for dialogue. But used as a disguised accusation, it only reinforces the very patterns you're trying to change. The key is self-awareness and intent: speak from your own experience, not as a way to control or correct the other person.

How to Structure an "I" Statement

A simple formula for crafting effective "I" statements is the following:

- **Start with "I feel":** Identify the emotion you are experiencing (e.g., frustrated or hurt).

- **Describe the behavior or situation:** Focus on the specific action or circumstance.

- **Explain why it matters to you:** Link your feelings to the impact of the behavior or situation.

There are also three key things you need to remember when crafting your "I" statement:

1. **Be specific:** Avoid vague complaints and focus on specific behaviors or situations.

2. **Stay neutral:** Keep your tone calm and avoid adding emotionally charged language.

3. **Focus on the present:** Discuss the current situation rather than dredging up past grievances.

Incorporating "I" Statements Into Negotiation

Using "I" statements during negotiations can help de-escalate tension and promote understanding. For instance, instead of saying "You're being unreasonable about the parenting schedule," say "I feel worried about how the current plan will affect the kids' stability." By framing your concerns in terms of your own experience, you create an opening for constructive dialogue rather than conflict.

I worked with a couple in mediation—Jack and Elise—who were negotiating the division of their shared property. One major sticking point was the family home. Jack wanted to sell it and split the proceeds, while Elise wanted to keep it for stability, especially for their teenage son, who had grown up in that house. Their conversations were fraught with accusations. Jack would say, "You're being selfish, holding on to that house just to spite me," and Elise would counter with, "You don't care about our son's well-being!"

Their interactions were so heated that it became impossible to make progress and each felt disrespected and disregarded by the other. I suggested they try expressing their concerns with "I" statements. Elise practiced saying, "I feel worried about our son's sense of stability if we sell the house because this is the only home he's ever known."

Jack was visibly less defensive when he heard this. While it took a few rounds for Jack to calm down, he eventually responded, "I didn't realize you were thinking about it from his perspective. I just feel overwhelmed by the financial burden of keeping the house."

By shifting their language and tone, they moved away from blame and toward understanding. This allowed them to explore creative options, like Elise keeping the house but refinancing it to remove Jack from the mortgage, which addressed both of their concerns.

Fostering collaboration begins with recognizing and addressing the other party's emotions.

Another powerful technique for fostering constructive communication is to find something you can agree with in the other person's perspective and use it as a springboard for collaboration.

"What I Like About Your Proposal..."

Inspired by Shirzad Chamine's work in *Positive Intelligence*, looking for common ground is an approach that validates the other party's ideas while keeping the conversation open to refinement. It's a simple yet effective way to defuse defensiveness and encourage joint problem-solving.

You begin by identifying an element of the other person's proposal that you genuinely appreciate or agree with. This could be the intention behind their idea, a specific detail in it, or even the effort they've made to consider a solution. It might be one little thing you can agree with, or it can be more. For example: "What I like about your proposal is that it prioritizes the kids' stability."

Next, you introduce additional possibilities by extending an invitation to expand or refine the idea collaboratively and frame it as a shared effort. For example you might say, "I wonder how we can maintain that stability and include flexibility for travel in the schedule?" Here's how that could play out.

Rachel and Sam were negotiating their parenting schedule. Rachel wanted a set routine to provide their children with stability, while Sam, who traveled frequently for work, wanted a more flexible arrangement. Their conversations were becoming increasingly tense, with both parties feeling unheard.

When Sam proposed a schedule that prioritized flexibility, Rachel initially resisted, feeling that it wouldn't provide the predictability the kids needed. Using the "What I like about your proposal" technique, I encouraged Rachel to respond differently.

Rachel began with "What I like about your proposal is that you're thinking about how to stay involved in the kids' lives even with your travel schedule." She then followed with "I wonder how we can incorporate that while also giving the kids a consistent routine at home?"

The tone of the conversation immediately shifted. Instead of feeling like adversaries, Rachel and Sam began exploring ways to integrate both of their priorities and with this felt relief that they could move from a competitive dynamic to one of collaboration. Ultimately, they developed a hybrid schedule that balanced flexibility and stability, satisfying both their concerns.

This approach defuses defensiveness by starting with validation, allowing the other party to feel heard and respected while lowering emotional barriers. It also encourages collaboration by framing your response as a "wonder" or "invitation," shifting the tone from opposition to partnership. In addition, focusing on shared goals rather than competing positions reframes the discussion, keeping it solution-oriented and constructive.

So make sure that you identify a specific element of the person's proposal that you truly appreciate because it is crucial you are genuine—insincerity will be acutely obvious. And neutral language is equally important, as phrases that sound dismissive (e.g., "That's an interesting idea, but...") can escalate tension.

This simple formula—acknowledge, then expand—can transform even the most contentious discussions into opportunities for creative problem-solving, helping both parties feel invested in the outcome. But sometimes the best response is to stay quiet.

The Power of Silence

As a teenager, sometimes I would approach my father with a problem, detailing my thoughts and frustrations. He would listen intently but remain silent. Eventually I would say, "Dad, did you hear me?" And he would reply, "Yes, I'm thinking about it."

His response always made me feel that my concerns were taken seriously. It wasn't just his words; the pause itself conveyed respect. His silence allowed me to express everything on my mind and fully articulate my struggles. Simultaneously, it indicated that he was thoughtfully considering my words before offering advice or opinions.

This simple habit taught me an invaluable lesson about communication: sometimes, silence is more powerful than words. Whether listening to a teenager's concerns or negotiating a divorce settlement, silence can foster deeper understanding and lead to more productive outcomes.

Silence is one of the most underrated tools in effective communication. Remaining silent after someone speaks encourages reflection and often prompts them to elaborate. This added insight can be crucial in grasping their true concerns, priorities, or hidden motivations. Instead of rushing to fill the silence with your own words, you create a space where they feel invited to share more openly.

In emotionally charged discussions, silence can also serve as a calming force. When tensions rise, pausing rather than reacting gives both parties a moment to reset emotionally. This brief break can defuse potential conflict, shifting the focus from escalation to problem-solving.

Silence signals thoughtfulness. Taking a moment before responding shows that you genuinely consider the other person's words. This reinforces the idea that their thoughts matter to you, fostering trust and encouraging a collaborative dynamic. A well-timed pause can transform the tone of the conversation, demonstrating your commitment to a constructive outcome.

By strategically embracing silence, you allow yourself time to think, give the other person a chance to feel heard, and create an opportunity for the conversation to advance with greater clarity and respect.

MASTERING THESE communication strategies—whether it's Powerful Non-Defensive Communication, reflective listening, tactical empathy, or well-crafted "I" statements—lays a strong foundation for reducing tension and nurturing a cooperative tone in your divorce negotiations. By creating a respectful environment where each party feels genuinely heard, you can stay focused on the core issues that matter most.

In the next chapter, I'll build on these techniques by exploring how to identify, articulate, and prioritize your real interests (introduced in chapter 2), giving you even greater clarity and leverage in your divorce negotiations.

KEY TAKEAWAYS

- **Maintain a respectful tone:** Stay calm to build trust and cooperation. Powerful Non-Defensive Communication—asking open-ended questions, using "I" statements, and confident vocal cues—also defuses tension.

- **Practice reflective listening:** Paraphrase and summarize to reduce misunderstandings and encourage constructive dialogue.

- **Apply tactical empathy:** Acknowledge emotions to build trust, lessen resistance, and shift from win-lose to collaborative solutions.

- **Use "I" statements and shared ideas:** Express your own experience to reduce blame and highlight aspects you like in the other's proposal to spark collaboration.

- **Leverage silence and empathy:** Pause intentionally to de-escalate tension, foster deeper understanding, and convert empathy into a strategic advantage.

7

Understanding Interests in Divorce Negotiations

NOW THAT you've learned how to communicate effectively, the next step is clarifying what truly matters to you. In negotiation, it's easy to get stuck on demands—but our demands are often surface-level positions. As I discussed in chapter 2, deeper *interests*—the needs, fears, and motivations driving those demands—are what truly shape decision-making. Understanding the difference between positions and interests allows for more creative and effective negotiations.

A demand is *what* you say you want, but an interest is *why* you want it.

For example, insisting on keeping the house might not just be about the property itself—it could be about preserving a sense of security or maintaining stability for your children. Identifying these underlying interests opens the door to alternative solutions that might serve you even better.

In this chapter, I'll delve into defining your interests more precisely than we did earlier in the book, uncovering your spouse's interests (even when they appear at odds with your own), and using this understanding to craft agreements that reflect what truly matters to you. I'll also introduce tools like reframing and the hypothesis of generosity, which can shift tense discussions from conflict to problem-solving.

Behind the Scenes

When going through a divorce, focusing on each party's deeper motivations—instead of just the demands each person brings to the table—can lead to more amicable and effective negotiations. Interests are the underlying reasons behind a position. They encompass the needs, desires, and concerns that drive your choices (and your ex's as well). Unlike positions, which are specific demands or solutions ("I want full custody" or "I want the house"), interests reveal the motivations behind the demands, and understanding them is crucial to achieving better outcomes.

Remember Marcy, who was determined to keep the house when she started working with me? She was angry at Steve for his choices and their impact on her life and the children's. She also worried her children would feel anxious and that her ability to be a good mother was under threat. To Marcy, staying in the house felt like the best way to protect her kids' sense of security. As you might recall, she also made a chart to identify her own interests and those she believed Steve had (chapter 3). Those "behind the scenes" reasons, the interests, are what truly drive negotiating positions—both yours and your ex's.

Divorce often creates anxiety and anger, so many of us naturally look for solutions that offer quick emotional relief in a challenging situation like divorce. Once we find something that we believe will ease our worries, we tend to cling to it—and that becomes our negotiating position. These positions can be very specific: "I want $5,000 in monthly alimony" or "I want full custody of the children." Although such demands may be the first thing to surface in negotiations, they can obscure the real interests behind them. Worse, positions are often rigid and encourage a false win-lose dynamic, which can derail any hope of collaboration.

Positions Versus Interests	
Position	**Interest**
I want the house.	I want stability for the children and continuity in their lives.
I want $5,000 a month in alimony.	I need financial security while I transition back into the workforce.
I want full custody of the children.	I am concerned about providing a stable environment for the kids.
I want the car.	I need reliable transportation for work and other daily responsibilities.
I don't want my ex to have any of our savings.	I am worried about having enough money for retirement and to cover future expenses.

The Four-Point Test for Interests

As you start thinking about potential solutions in your divorce negotiations, make a list of your own interests to guide the process. Each interest will be most useful if it meets the following criteria developed by Gary J. Friedman and Jack Himmelstein as part of their Understanding-Based Model of mediation:

1 **Emotional resonance:** It's something you genuinely care about.

2 **Multiple options:** It points to more than one possible solution (not overly specific).

3 **Tangibility:** It's concrete enough to be acted upon rather than just a vague desire.

4 **Positive framing:** It focuses on what *you* need instead of what your ex should lose.

Take, for example, ensuring "a stable environment for the children." This concern resonates emotionally, reflecting a deep concern for the children's well-being. It also allows for multiple options, such as shared custody arrangements, maintaining the family home, or selecting a school district that suits both parents. The interest is tangible, focusing on the clear and specific objective of stability, and it is framed as a benefit for the children's lives rather than as a gain for one parent at the other's expense.

In contrast, a goal like "I want the car" might fail this test by being too narrow and focusing on a single possession instead of the deeper need—reliable transportation. Similarly, "I don't want my ex to get any of our savings" is about depriving the other person rather than ensuring a specific benefit for yourself.

Once you've run your interests through the test, do the same exercise for your spouse. Marcy did this beautifully when she wrote that one thing that was important to Steve was to have common interests with his life partner. She recognized that this was something that had broken down in her marriage and that it was a very important interest of his.

Finding out *why* your spouse values certain outcomes can help you shape proposals that address their underlying concerns as well as yours. One way to find out what is important to your spouse is to ask them. Marcy could ask Steve, "What matters to you when you think about the best outcome around the house?" This inquiry is a good example of how she might find out more information about Steve's priorities. Similarly, you can ask your ex what it is that is important to them around an issue that is important to you. But be sure to adopt a calm tone and open body language—and be genuinely curious. If you take this approach, you can discover your ex's real motivations, making it easier to find common ground.

The Hypothesis of Generosity

Most people view themselves as good, ethical individuals. Yet, during a divorce, it's common to attribute your spouse's actions to malicious intent and make the assumption they're out to punish or harm you. This is a classic example of the fundamental attribution error—blaming someone's character ("they're spiteful!") rather than considering that their actions may stem from their own needs or fears.

While it's possible that someone might occasionally act out of revenge, more often each spouse is simply aiming to secure what matters most to them: maintaining financial stability, preserving a relationship with the children, or holding on to a newfound personal freedom. These goals can feel threatening, but they're often not a deliberate attack on you.

The "hypothesis of generosity," a term popularized by the Harvard Negotiation Project in the book *Difficult Conversations*, encourages a more constructive perspective. It invites you to assume your ex's behavior is driven primarily by their own needs or challenges rather than intentional malice. For instance, if they're pushing for personal freedom, it may be about their own journey—and probably not about you, or even with the intent to cause hurt, at all.

When you acknowledge that your spouse's words and actions may be more about fulfilling their needs than inflicting pain on you, you can craft proposals that consider their underlying interests and, ultimately, increase your chances of reaching an agreement that also satisfies yours. When you avoid attributing every action to spite, communication tends to improve and you're better positioned to negotiate with clarity and empathy.

It's also possible that your spouse might hear *your* interests as an attack on them. This disconnect can feel deeply frustrating when all you're trying to do is express legitimate concerns. Misunderstandings like these happen all the time in divorce negotiations. Reframing can bridge this gap.

Reframing Your Perspective for Constructive Dialogue

At its core, reframing involves looking at a situation—or a statement—from a different angle and shifting the tone away from strict positions and conflict to underlying interests and solutions. Reframing allows

The "hypothesis of generosity" invites you to assume your ex's behavior is driven primarily by their own needs or challenges rather than intentional malice.

both perspectives to be included, easing the competitive dynamic and fostering more productive discussions. While the hypothesis of generosity helps you see your ex's motives through a more empathetic lens, reframing is how you demonstrate that understanding in the negotiation itself.

Imagine a scenario where one spouse insists, "I need the house because I want our children to stay with me." The other spouse may interpret this as a power grab or an attempt to control the situation, leading to feelings of resentment and a breakdown in communication. However, through reframing, you could present the same concern differently, saying, "I believe it's important for the kids to feel stable and secure in their environment. How can we make sure they have continuity in their lives?"

This reframed statement focuses on shared interests—what's best for the children—rather than rigid demands, allowing for more open, cooperative discussions. The conversation shifts from adversarial to collaborative, making it easier to work toward mutually acceptable solutions. Reframing is not just about changing the words you use—it's about adopting a mindset of collaboration, where both parties' interests are acknowledged and valued. Try this brief exercise to help you get comfortable with reframing.

1. **Identify a contentious point:** Think of a topic that feels fraught or one where you've felt misunderstood.

2. **Write down your current framing:** Take note of how you typically express your concerns.

3. **Reframe with underlying interests:** Shift the focus to your underlying interests and consider the other party's interests.

4. **Reflect on the impact:** Consider how the reframed statement might change the tone of the conversation and help you collaborate rather than clash.

In the following table, I present a few snapshots of how reframing can soften a rigid position and invite a more productive exchange:

What You Want to Say	What Your Ex Might Hear	Reframing Your Interest
"I want more time with the kids to stay involved in their daily lives."	You're trying to take the kids away from them.	"I believe it's important for the kids to have strong relationships with both of us. How can we create a schedule that supports that?"
"I need to keep the house because it's important for the kids' stability."	You want the house to gain an advantage over them.	"Stability for the kids really matters to me. What are some ways we can make sure they feel secure, wherever they live?"
"I need financial support to maintain my current standard of living."	You're trying to take advantage of them financially.	"I'd like to find a financial arrangement where we both feel stable and secure as we move forward."
"I want to continue being part of the kids' school and extracurricular activities."	You think they don't care about the kids' activities.	"Let's talk about how we can both stay actively involved in the kids' school and activities so they feel supported by both of us."

Reframing Your Spouse's Perspective

If you are struggling to think about your spouse's perspective separate from an attack on you, here are some ways to think about this.

- When you hear your spouse say something like "You're just trying to take the kids away from me," it may indicate that they feel threatened about losing their relationship with the children. To address this concern, you might reframe your response along the lines of, "It sounds like you're worried about your connection with the kids. How can we both remain active and present in their lives?"

- If you encounter a statement such as "You're only interested in the money," this could suggest that your spouse feels insecure about their own financial future. A helpful reply could be, "I sense that financial security is important to you. Let's talk about how we can both achieve stability after the divorce."

- If your spouse says "You never listen to my concerns," that may indicate that they feel unheard or dismissed. In this situation, you could respond by saying, "It sounds like you want to make sure your concerns are acknowledged. What's the most important issue we should focus on?"

- Similarly, if your spouse says "You always make decisions without me," they may be communicating a sense of exclusion from the decision-making process. You can acknowledge this by offering, "I understand you want to be involved in decision-making. How can we create a process that ensures we both have a say?"

- Finally, if you hear them say "You're just being difficult to get back at me," it might mean your spouse perceives the negotiation as driven by past grievances. A compassionate way to respond is by reframing: "It sounds like you're feeling hurt. How can we focus on finding solutions that work for both of us?"

By presenting each statement, considering what it might really mean for your spouse, and offering a reframed response, you can shift the conversation from defensiveness to a more empathetic, solution-focused dialogue.

Another way to consider your spouse's perspective is to ask yourself, What would I be thinking or feeling if I were in their shoes? That tactic helped me in my own divorce when I was once late dropping off my kids because the traffic was terrible. My ex accused me of interfering with his parenting time, and I felt unfairly judged and defensive. But when I imagined myself in his place—worried about losing valuable time with the kids—I realized his anxiety was about preserving his relationship with them, not an attack on me personally. Responding with that in mind allowed me to address his real concern, defuse the tension, and find a scheduling adjustment that worked for both of us.

This wasn't easy for me. I was angry and insulted that he could think I was intentionally trying to interfere. Over time, I came to realize he was dysregulated by the divorce. His world felt upside down, and I had played a role in causing that upheaval, so it was no wonder he lacked sympathy for my struggles with traffic.

Reframing isn't about conceding your needs; it's about presenting them in a way that makes others more likely to listen. By replacing a power-driven or blame-focused dynamic with a tone of curiosity, empathy, and cooperation, both sides can feel heard, which sets the stage for more equitable solutions.

WITH A CLEARER SENSE of your interests and practical ways to reframe tough conversations, you're ready to take your negotiation skills to the next level. In the upcoming chapters, let's build on these tools and explore additional techniques that will empower you to navigate complex dynamics and craft outcomes aligned with your core values and goals.

KEY TAKEAWAYS

- **Focus on underlying interests rather than rigid positions:** Because surface demands (positions) often mask your and your spouse's deeper fears and needs (interests), try to shift the focus to the interests.

- **Use the four-point test:** Deploy emotional resonance, multiple options, tangibility, and positive framing to clarify how genuine your interests are.

- **Apply the "hypothesis of generosity":** Assume that your spouse's actions stem from their own anxieties, not malice.

- **Reframe rigid statements:** Emphasize shared goals and seek collaborative solutions.

- **Cultivate empathy and curiosity:** Learn more about your spouse's perspective to reduce defensiveness and open pathways to mutual agreement.

8

Building Your Strategy: The Best and the Worst Alternatives

NOW THAT you've got a solid handle on identifying interests and reframing the conversation, it's time to put that knowledge into action. Negotiating a divorce settlement can feel overwhelming, but having the right strategies in place can help you advocate for what matters most while keeping discussions productive.

Think of all the techniques I'm about to explore with you in the next chapters as tools in your negotiation tool kit. The more prepared you are, the better equipped you'll be to avoid getting stuck in endless back-and-forth discussions or feeling pressured into an unfair agreement.

Let's begin with BATNA and WATNA—two essential concepts that will help you make informed decisions throughout the process. You might have heard the terms BATNA and WATNA thrown around in negotiation discussions, but what do they really mean?

- **BATNA (Best Alternative to a Negotiated Agreement):** This is your backup plan if negotiations fall apart. If you and your spouse can't agree, what's your next best option? Knowing this helps you avoid accepting a bad deal out of fear.

- **WATNA (Worst Alternative to a Negotiated Agreement):** This is the worst-case scenario if you walk away from negotiations. Understanding this prevents you from overestimating your leverage and making risky choices.

Divorce negotiations aren't just about what you want; they're about what's realistic. Knowing your BATNA gives you confidence, while understanding your WATNA keeps you grounded in the risks of walking away. I'm going to use the following real-world example to illustrate how these concepts play out in a divorce negotiation.

Gabriel and Eva: Considering Best and Worst Alternatives

Gabriel comes from a wealthy family where signing a prenuptial agreement is a long-standing tradition. These were the main terms of his prenuptial agreement:

- Gabriel's inherited and gifted wealth remains his separate property.
- Spousal support is limited to a share of Gabriel's earned income.

As an artist, Gabriel's income would likely always be modest. Even though his and his spouse's lifestyle would be largely supported by income from Gabriel's family's assets, those funds were deemed by the prenup to be off-limits in the event of divorce.

When Gabriel and Eva married, Eva willingly signed the prenuptial agreement without dwelling too much on the details. At the time, the couple were deeply in love and the idea of planning for a potential divorce felt unnecessary. Twenty years later, after building a family together, Gabriel and Eva decide to divorce. Gabriel has already gifted Eva some of his separate money, but it's not enough to sustain the lifestyle they've shared to date. Gabriel genuinely wants to be generous, but his idea of generosity does not align with Eva's expectations, leaving them at an impasse. Let's consider the BATNAs and WATNAs of each individual.

Evaluating Eva's BATNA and WATNA

Eva must consider both her best and worst alternatives if negotiations fail.

Eva's BATNA: Legally, her position is weak due to the prenuptial agreement, which limits her financial claims. However, she could consider challenging the prenup on grounds of unconscionability or lack of full disclosure. While that challenge is unlikely to succeed, it might create uncertainty for Gabriel, encouraging him to offer a more generous settlement. From a non-legal perspective, Eva could also focus on creating financial independence for herself by exploring career opportunities or entrepreneurial ventures that provide long-term stability.

Eva's WATNA: If negotiations break down and the prenup is fully enforced, she will receive only minimal spousal support and little to no share of Gabriel's wealth. A prolonged legal battle could drain her resources and strain co-parenting relationships, making it difficult for her to move forward constructively.

Eva's strategic steps: To strengthen her position without escalating conflict, Eva can do the following:

1 Assess the prenup's legal viability: Consult an attorney about whether she has a case to challenge the agreement, even if only as a negotiation tool.

2 Signal, but not commit to, legal action: Suggest that she is considering legal options (without immediately pursuing them) to create leverage.

3 Highlight the cost of litigation: Emphasize to Gabriel that a court battle would be costly, emotionally taxing, and potentially damaging to his reputation.

4. Appeal to Gabriel's values: Frame her requests in ways that align with his self-perception as a fair and generous person.

5. Propose mediation or collaborative negotiation: Suggest an alternative resolution process that allows Gabriel to avoid public disputes and maintain family harmony.

Evaluating Gabriel's BATNA and WATNA

Although Gabriel holds legal leverage in this divorce negotiation, he must also weigh the risks of his situation.

Gabriel's BATNA: He would likely win if he were to enforce the pre-nuptial agreement in court. But he might consider offering Eva a pre-emptive settlement to avoid legal action while still protecting his wealth.

Gabriel's WATNA: If Eva were to challenge the prenup, this would likely create prolonged litigation and uncertainty. He could also sustain damage to his reputation within his family or community, particularly if he were seen as being unfair or ungenerous. Litigation would also strain their co-parenting and increase emotional distress for both parties.

Gabriel's strategic steps: To protect himself while maintaining control over the negotiation, Gabriel can consider the following:

1. Consider pre-emptive generosity: He could voluntarily offer Eva a lump sum or assets to avoid the risk of litigation.

2. Use private negotiation methods: Use mediation to keep divorce discussions out of court.

3. Propose conditional settlements: Offering financial security to Eva in exchange for a waiver of legal challenges.

4. Balance legal defense with strategy: Finally, Gabriel might opt to defend the prenuptial agreement while signaling his openness to negotiation with Eva.

The Decision Tree Process

Once you have a clear understanding of your BATNA and WATNA, as well as those of your spouse, the next step is to map out how these alternatives can influence your decision-making process. A decision tree is a practical tool that can help you visualize and navigate the various possible outcomes of your negotiation, providing a structured way to assess your options as you choose which path forward is best.

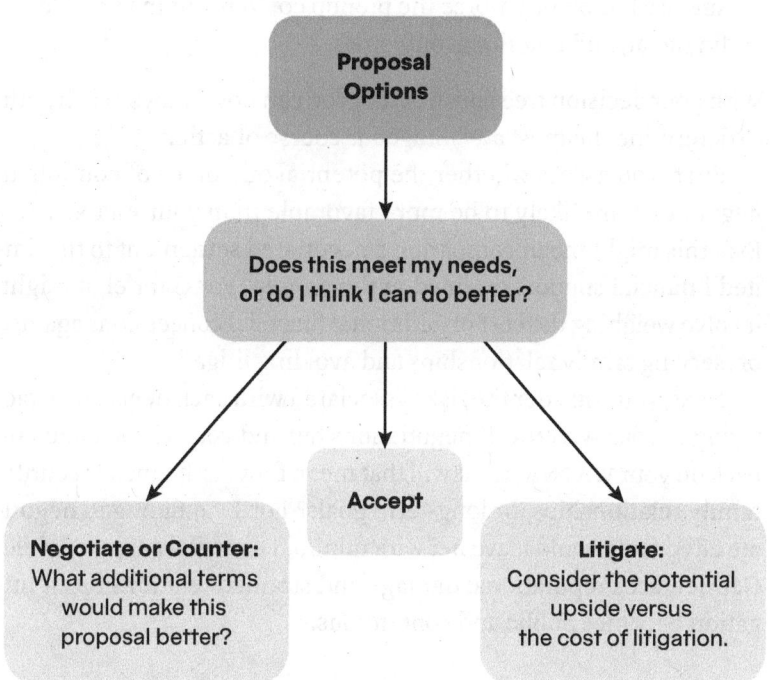

Again, I'll use the example of Gabriel and Eva to showcase this tool.

You start the decision tree by identifying the key decision points in your negotiation. The decision tree will branch out from these decision points, showing the potential outcomes of each choice.

- **Initial decision point:** The first branch of your decision tree begins with the choice between continuing negotiations or pursuing your BATNA. For instance, Eva might decide whether to push Gabriel for a more generous settlement or to prepare for the potential of going to court.

- **Outcome branches:** Each decision leads to several possible outcomes. If Eva continues negotiating, she might reach a compromise that improves her financial security or face a breakdown in talks, defaulting to her WATNA. Similarly, Gabriel's choice to pursue mediation or enforce the prenup could result in varied legal, financial, and emotional outcomes.

With your decision tree constructed, you can now analyze each path to determine the most advantageous course of action.

First, you assess whether the potential outcomes of continued negotiation are likely to be more favorable than your BATNA. For Eva, this might mean comparing a negotiated settlement to the limited financial support outlined in the prenup. For Gabriel, it might involve weighing the cost of additional financial concessions against preserving family relationships and avoiding litigation.

Next, you consider the risks associated with each decision by factoring in your WATNA. If negotiations fail and you are forced to fall back on your WATNA, what will that mean for your financial security, family relationships, or long-term goals? For Eva, failing to negotiate effectively could leave her with minimal financial support, while Gabriel faces reputational damage and strained relationships if litigation becomes public and contentious.

Balancing and Adjusting Your Strategy

The decision tree allows you to visualize and balance your BATNA and WATNA against various negotiation outcomes, helping you decide when to compromise, hold firm, or change strategies altogether.

Divorce negotiations aren't just about what you want; they're about what's realistic.

To mitigate risks—reducing the fallout of your WATNA—Gabriel might offer a fair settlement to avoid a costly court battle, while Eva could focus on creative solutions to improve her chances of securing a better outcome without litigation. At the same time, both parties can use the decision tree to uncover opportunities that strengthen their BATNA. For example, if Eva recognizes that Gabriel values discretion and family harmony, she may leverage those priorities to negotiate a more favorable settlement.

Negotiations are fluid, and your decision tree should be revisited regularly as circumstances change. With new information, shifts in the other party's stance, or evolving priorities on your end, you may need to refine your approach. Updating the decision tree involves adjusting it to reflect emerging alternatives.

For example, if Gabriel signals a willingness to mediate, Eva might focus on compromise instead of litigation. By continuously revisiting the decision tree, you ensure that your strategy remains dynamic and responsive, better positioning you to stay ahead of potential challenges and take advantage of new opportunities as they arise.

AS YOU MOVE INTO the structured phase of negotiation, it's important to remember that your emotions are playing a significant role in how the discussions unfold. Now is a good time to take steps to manage your emotional responses to help you stay grounded and focused on the bigger picture and help give you insights on what is happening for you and the other person in your negotiation.

Managing Your Emotional Responses in Negotiations

Even with clear strategies and plans, moments of stress or frustration may arise, especially when dealing with critical issues. Here are three strategies to help you calm yourself. You can also look at appendix 2 for a list of exercises to assist you in regulating your emotions if you need some more ideas.

1. **Breathing exercises:** Breathing exercises help calm the nervous system, allowing you to regain focus and clarity and stay present for the conversation. When you feel anxiety or tension rising, pause and take a few deep breaths, exhaling slowly after each deep inhale. There are lots of resources available for those wanting to help ground themselves with breathing exercises. Find one that works for you, and don't forget to breathe.

2. **Emotional objectivity:** William Ury, co-author of the influential book *Getting to Yes*, encourages imagining yourself as if you're on a negotiation stage, while simultaneously sending part of your attention to a "mental and emotional balcony." From this vantage point, he explains, you can maintain a sense of calm, keep a broader perspective, and stay firmly focused on what truly matters. Going to your mental and emotional "balcony" helps prevent any immediate reactions to emotionally charged statements, giving you the space to think strategically rather than reactively.

3. **Breaks:** Don't hesitate to request short breaks during high-stress moments. Take a bio break, get a cup of tea, or walk the surroundings for fifteen to twenty minutes. Breaks like these can prevent emotional escalation and give both parties time to reflect and recenter before continuing.

UNDERSTANDING BATNA and WATNA is not just about knowing your fallback options—it's about using them strategically to negotiate from a position of strength. By balancing legal and practical considerations, both Eva and Gabriel can work toward a solution that minimizes conflict while protecting their interests. You can do this too.

By mapping out alternatives and leveraging key strategies, you can navigate divorce negotiations with confidence and purpose. Now you are ready to make a proposal, and that's what we'll explore in the next chapter.

KEY TAKEAWAYS

- **Recognize the power of BATNA and WATNA:** Understanding these fallback positions if negotiations fail fosters confident decision-making and helps you avoid unfavorable deals.

- **Evaluate your negotiation position:** Assess your legal rights, financial options, and leverage. Exploring strategies like making legal challenges or improving your personal finances strengthens your bargaining power.

- **Consider both sides:** Every negotiation involves risks. Balancing your BATNA and WATNA with the other party's possible outcomes supports mutually beneficial proposals.

- **Use the decision tree process:** Mapping your outcomes clarifies when you should compromise, hold firm, or pivot, ensuring an informed, flexible negotiation process.

- **Manage your emotions strategically:** Techniques like deep breathing, perspective-shifting, and short breaks maintain calm and keep you focused on key interests.

9

The Proposal Blueprint

NOW THAT you've developed a strong foundation in understanding interests, reflective listening, framing and reframing, BATNA and WATNA, decision trees, and identifying the key issues to negotiate, you're ready to move into the next critical phase: outlining how the proposals will be made. This is where all your preparation comes to life—where strategy meets action.

The proposal process is about more than just deciding what to ask for. It's about crafting how and when you present your proposals in a way that resonates with your ex and aligns with your goals. Thoughtful timing, strategic anchoring, compelling storytelling, and the offer of meaningful choices can make the difference between a productive conversation and a frustrating deadlock. By approaching this phase with care and strategy, you not only increase your chances of achieving a favorable outcome but you also lay the groundwork for a smoother post-divorce relationship.

Before diving into the specifics, let's clarify a few key terms that will guide you through the rest of the chapter.

- **Proposal:** The proposal is a single idea or offer—like a suggested parenting schedule or a specific spousal support amount.

- **Package:** A group of proposals presented together, reflecting how different parts of the agreement interact.

- **MESO (Multiple Equivalent Simultaneous Offer):** A powerful method of presenting several different packages at once—each equally acceptable to you but structured differently to appeal to your spouse's preferences.

As you read, you'll see how these tools build on one another to help you craft flexible, well-timed offers that support your goals.

Negotiation isn't just a transactional process; it's an emotional one. Proposals carry weight—they signal what you value, how you perceive the other person's needs, and your willingness to collaborate. This chapter will guide you through structuring proposals with both strategy and empathy, ensuring you approach this phase with confidence and clarity. Timing is everything in negotiation. When (and how) you present your proposal can be just as important as what you propose. Well-timed proposals not only show thoughtfulness but also leverage the emotional and practical state of the negotiation, increasing the likelihood of a positive response.

Make the First Proposal

Whenever possible, aim to be the one who makes the first proposal. The party who makes the first offer often has the advantage of setting the tone and framework for the negotiation. This is known as *anchoring* because you are establishing a reference point that will likely shape how subsequent proposals are evaluated.

A well-crafted anchor not only sets the stage for the conversation but also creates a range that is favorable to you. For example, if you're negotiating spousal support, an initial proposal of a specific amount establishes a starting point that the other party is likely to negotiate around. This can subtly influence the trajectory of the entire discussion by framing what's "reasonable" in terms of your own goals.

Anchoring effectively requires balance. If your proposal is perceived as overly aggressive, it risks being dismissed outright and eroding trust. Instead, frame your anchor as fair and reasonable while still advancing your interests. Highlight how it aligns with legal standards, financial realities, or shared goals. Finally, remember that anchoring is most effective when supported by careful preparation. Before making your first offer, gather enough information about the other party's priorities, BATNA, and WATNA to ensure your proposal is both strategically advantageous and grounded in reality.

Violet and Kevin are negotiating spousal support as part of their divorce settlement. Violet, who has been the primary caregiver for their two young children, is worried about maintaining stability for herself and the kids. Kevin, a financial analyst, wants to ensure that any support arrangement is manageable given his career fluctuations.

Instead of making a vague or extreme proposal, Violet takes a strategic approach. She prepares by researching typical support amounts based on income and child-related expenses. When making the first proposal, Violet suggests a monthly amount that is slightly higher than what she realistically expects, while clearly explaining that this figure accounts for the children's school costs and basic living expenses.

By doing so, Violet sets an anchor that makes room for negotiation while appearing reasonable and fair. Kevin, seeing that Violet's proposal is based on thoughtful consideration rather than pure self-interest, responds with a counteroffer rather than outright rejection. This approach keeps the conversation focused and collaborative rather than combative.

Why Anchoring Matters

Anchoring isn't just about numbers—it's also about how you present your proposal. Framing the first offer in a way that positions you as *proactive* and *solutions-oriented* helps set a constructive tone for the negotiation. For instance, instead of simply proposing a percentage split of marital property, you could present options for dividing specific assets (like real estate, retirement accounts, and liquid funds) that demonstrate thoughtfulness and fairness. Anchoring is crucial for a few reasons.

- **Shaping expectations:** Your proposal is the initial reference point, influencing how reasonable other offers appear.
- **Psychological impact:** People often frame their thinking around the first offer—even if they initially object—making it harder for them to deviate too far from that anchor.
- **Positioning:** Being the first to propose signals confidence and preparation, which can foster a more collaborative and constructive tone.

While making the first offer can be highly advantageous, it's important to anchor strategically and avoid pitfalls. Here are a few points to keep in mind before you make an offer.

- **Make it credible:** Your anchor should be grounded in reality and supported by data, legal benchmarks, or clear reasoning. For example, if you are proposing a spousal support figure, reference your living expenses or income disparity when proposing spousal support.
- **Be mindful of your tone:** A proposal that feels overly aggressive or disconnected from the other party's priorities may spark resistance or shut down communication. Strive for a balance of firmness and empathy.
- **Stay flexible:** If your first anchor proposal is rejected outright, remember the goal is to foster productive dialogue rather than forcing an ultimatum.

Anchoring is about creating a framework that aligns with your goals while shaping the negotiation's trajectory. By combining thoughtful numbers with a solutions-oriented presentation, you not only strengthen your position, you also guide the conversation toward a resolution that works for you and your spouse.

The Timing of Your Proposal

As I mentioned earlier, getting your proposal in first to anchor the negotiation is a positive strategic move as you'll shaping the initial steps of the negotiations. However, thoughtful timing demonstrates that you've taken the time to gather relevant information and align your suggestions with the current context of the negotiation. Present your proposals only after you've developed a clear understanding of your spouse's interests, priorities, and BATNA, but avoid waiting so long that frustration builds or your spouse feels compelled to seize control by making the first offer themselves.

Effective timing considers both the emotional state of your spouse and the practical circumstances of the negotiation. For example, if your spouse has expressed anxiety about finding stable housing post-divorce, present a proposal that addresses their concern—such as helping them secure a down payment or temporary financial support. This proposal could meet their immediate need while advancing your long-term goals. It also shows empathy and builds goodwill, increasing the likelihood of acceptance.

Presenting proposals too early or too late carries risks. Premature proposals may lack the benefit of fully understanding the other party's interests, priorities, or BATNA, which can result in an offer that is either unrealistic or poorly aligned with the dynamics of the negotiation. Conversely, delaying too long can frustrate the other person or allow them to establish the negotiation's framework on their terms. Many people believe that compromise is the key to achieving the best result, so they'll present a proposal as soon as they can. However, there are three significant risks in proposing a compromise too early.

1 **The other party treats your compromise as an opening offer:** The other party may treat your thoughtful compromise as merely the opening round in competitive bargaining, using it as a baseline from which to demand more. Remember Eva and Gabriel discussing the division of assets while considering their prenuptial

agreement? If Eva were to offer a compromise proposal early in the process, hoping to move quickly toward resolution, Gabriel could see this as a signal that she is willing to concede further and he might respond with additional demands. This dynamic can leave the person offering the compromise feeling demoralized and exposed, as their willingness to be reasonable is misinterpreted as a sign of weakness.

2. **You have incomplete information:** Proposing a compromise before fully understanding the external reality—such as legal standards, financial constraints, or logistical considerations—can result in an offer that is unworkable or unrealistic. For instance, offering a specific spousal support figure without a clear understanding of both parties' financial situations may backfire if it is later revealed that the figure is unsustainable or insufficient.

3. **You misjudge what is important to the other party:** If your assumptions about the other party's priorities are incorrect, an early compromise is likely to unintentionally offend or alienate them. A proposal that fails to address what they value most may be perceived as dismissive or insulting, causing the negotiation to stall or even regress. For example, if Gabriel places a high emotional value on retaining a family property, and Eva proposes selling it as part of an early compromise, Gabriel may feel disregarded, setting the negotiation back rather than moving it forward.

To avoid these pitfalls, it's crucial to strike a balance between patience and preparation. Take the time to gather the information you need, understand the other party's priorities, and align your proposals with your overarching goals. Compromise should be introduced only when the negotiation is at a stage where both parties are invested in finding a solution and the groundwork has been laid for mutual understanding.

Proposals presented at the right time can create momentum in the negotiation. For instance, after a productive conversation where your ex has shared their priorities, you could follow up with proposals that align with those priorities, demonstrating that you've been actively listening and incorporating their input. This not only builds trust but also encourages them to stay engaged in the process.

Let's say that Eva knows Gabriel is feeling pressure from his family to finalize the divorce amicably and avoid negative publicity. Eva could time her proposals to coincide with this external pressure, presenting multiple options that reflect her needs while subtly alleviating Gabriel's concerns about reputational damage. For instance, she might propose asset division options that emphasize privacy and discretion, framing her approach as cooperative and mutually respectful.

Further Timing Considerations

To ensure your proposals are well timed, consider these questions:

- Have you identified your ex's most pressing concerns or interests?
- Do you understand their BATNA and WATNA?
- Is the other party in a good place—both emotionally and logistically—to receive and evaluate your proposals constructively?
- Are you choosing a moment when they're likely to feel engaged and collaborative rather than defensive or resistant?

Be prepared to adjust your timing based on unexpected developments. If new information emerges—such as a sudden change in your ex's priorities—consider accelerating or revising your proposal to address the shift. For example, if Gabriel unexpectedly decides he wants to keep a particular property for sentimental reasons, Eva might revise her asset division MESOs to include options that allow him to retain that property while meeting her financial needs elsewhere.

Timing isn't just about avoiding mistakes—it's about leveraging your opportunities to guide the negotiation toward a favorable outcome. However, the *way* you present your proposal is just as important as *when* you present it.

A well-crafted anchor
not only sets the stage for
the conversation but
also creates a range that
is favorable to you.

Structuring Proposals as Packages

When negotiating divorce terms, it's essential to remember that no issue exists in isolation. Parenting plans, asset division, and financial support are all interconnected. While the ultimate goal is to create a comprehensive package that addresses these key areas, it's important not to rush this process. Each issue must be considered thoughtfully, with both parties' interests carefully examined before combining them into packages.

There's a risk in moving too quickly to package proposals, as it can lead to overlooking important details or failing to fully address each person's concerns. Taking the time to understand the priorities and interests behind each issue ensures that the final package is both fair and sustainable. I'll talk more about why structuring proposals as packages is important later in this chapter.

Once you've fully explored each topic, packaging proposals becomes an effective way to balance trade-offs and create solutions that feel comprehensive rather than piecemeal. For example, if you're discussing both custody and support, you might propose a schedule that allows more parenting time for one party in exchange for a different financial arrangement.

Packaging proposals thoughtfully encourages flexibility and collaboration while ensuring that no critical issue is overlooked or rushed. Once you've developed thoughtful proposals and considered how they work together as packages, you can begin presenting them in a way that offers flexibility and reduces resistance. One of the most effective methods for doing this is the MESO—Multiple Equivalent Simultaneous Offers—approach, flexible options that give your spouse the power to choose while ensuring your priorities stay intact.

The MESO Method

When negotiating, presenting the other person with choices can be a powerful way for you to foster your collaboration and reduce their resistance. One effective method is to use MESOs (Multiple Equivalent Simultaneous Offers)—a negotiation tactic developed through the research of Professor Victoria Husted Medvec and Adam Galinsky, and discussed in Medvec's terrific book *Negotiate Without Fear*. This approach involves presenting several different proposals simultaneously. Each proposal is equally valuable to you but structured differently to offer your spouse flexibility and options.

For example, if your goal is to achieve a fifty-fifty custody arrangement, you could propose several different schedules that meet this goal while offering flexibility for your spouse to choose between them. As an example, here are some suggestions that meet that guideline:

- **Week-on/week-off schedule:** Each parent alternates full weeks, ensuring equal time and a consistent routine.

- **5/5/2/2 schedule:** One parent has Monday and Tuesday, the other has Wednesday and Thursday, and weekends (including Friday) alternate, offering frequent transitions but maintaining balance.

- **Monthly split:** Custody alternates in month-long intervals, allowing for more extended periods of time with each parent.

- **Seasonal schedule:** One schedule for the school year (e.g., weekdays with one parent and weekends with the other) and a different one for summer, balancing both academic consistency and vacation flexibility.

Each of these options achieves your goal of fifty-fifty time while providing your spouse with choices that account for their different preferences or logistical considerations. By offering this variety, you demonstrate thoughtfulness and collaboration, reducing resistance and increasing the likelihood of reaching an agreement.

The MESO in Action

Now, let's revisit Eva and Gabriel's scenario again to show you how MESOs can balance the couple's competing priorities while fostering a spirit of cooperation and thoughtfulness between them.

Eva and Gabriel's financial negotiation is complex due to the constraints of their prenuptial agreement and Gabriel's stated desire to be generous but within limits. Eva decides to use the MESO method not just to offer choices but to appeal to Gabriel's need to maintain control and minimize conflict. So she crafts three different packages for his consideration:

1. **The stability package:** Eva receives a lump-sum payment that provides her with immediate financial security, allowing Gabriel to retain ownership of their real estate portfolio without ongoing financial obligations. This option emphasizes closure and simplicity.

2. **The partnership package:** Eva retains partial ownership of their vacation home, with an agreement to co-manage it for five years before selling and splitting the proceeds. This option highlights their shared history and a collaborative approach to maintaining the property's value.

3. **The long-term security package:** Eva receives a larger share of retirement accounts, ensuring her future financial stability, while Gabriel keeps the vacation home and other real estate assets intact. This option aligns with Gabriel's preference for retaining properties that hold emotional and family significance.

So what are the strategic benefits of these packages to Gabriel?

- **They appeal to Gabriel's values:** Each package reflects Gabriel's desire to maintain a positive post-divorce relationship while offering clear pathways to preserve his financial autonomy.

- **They reduce his resistance:** Presenting multiple options empowers Gabriel to feel more in control of the decision-making process, reducing the likelihood of outright rejection.

- **They balance logic and emotion:** The stability package appeals to logic and efficiency, the partnership package appeals to their shared history, and the long-term security package appeals to fairness and Gabriel's emotional and family ties to the properties.

With these packages, Eva not only provides viable pathways to resolution but she also frames herself as a thoughtful and reasonable negotiator and increases the chances of an amicable settlement. The case story of Eva and Gabriel demonstrates how the MESO method can create opportunities for flexibility and collaboration in even the most complex negotiations. But to fully harness the potential of MESOs, it's important to understand the benefits they offer and how to craft them effectively.

Why MESOs Are Effective in Divorce

MESOs can greatly enhance divorce negotiations. By presenting multiple equally valuable proposals, you engage the other party in a more collaborative process, minimize resistance, and increase satisfaction with the outcome. This approach reframes the conversation from a yes-or-no decision to one that asks "which option works best for both of us?"—a shift that fosters genuine problem-solving. Here are the key benefits of MESOs:

- **They shift the dynamic to collaboration:** Presenting several options focuses on finding solutions rather than determining a "winner." This approach reduces defensiveness and keeps attention on shared objectives. For example, Eva might say to Gabriel, "I've thought about what's most important to both of us and have a few ideas I'd love your thoughts on," emphasizing her interest in balanced outcomes.

- **They encourage constructive dialogue:** Offering choices replaces "agree or disagree" with "which option best fits our needs?" People who feel heard and valued remain more engaged. If Gabriel sees that Eva respects his concerns—such as preserving inherited assets—he's more likely to reciprocate by meeting her needs in return.

- **They promote flexibility and goodwill:** Providing multiple proposals shows openness to collaboration, which often prompts the other party to respond fairly. If Gabriel perceives Eva's suggestions as equitable, he's more inclined to negotiate productively.

- **They help resolve individual issues:** When the other person senses a genuine effort toward fairness, they're often more receptive overall. If Gabriel trusts that Eva's asset-division proposals reflect consideration for his priorities, he's more apt to collaborate on other topics like child custody or support.

- **They foster shared ownership of solutions:** Allowing the other person to select from various options boosts their sense of agency. This co-creation reduces post-agreement resentment and encourages a healthier long-term relationship. By leveraging MESOs, you promote respect, creativity, and mutual problem-solving—vital elements for a durable, cooperative agreement.

When you incorporate MESOs into your negotiation strategy, you create a constructive environment that supports both parties' interests, paving the way for lasting and mutually satisfactory resolutions.

Crafting MESOs in Divorce

To use MESOs effectively, there are several key points of preparation you should consider:

- **Take time to understand your spouse's interests:** Before presenting your proposals, gather information about your spouse's priorities, concerns, and interests. For instance, Eva's proposals should reflect her understanding that Gabriel values retaining control over his inherited assets while maintaining a positive post-divorce relationship.

- **Maintain equal value in each offer:** Ensure that each offer is equally advantageous to you, even if structured differently. This allows you to stay aligned with your own goals while providing genuine flexibility to the other party.

- **Frame proposals constructively:** Highlight how each option addresses their needs. For example, Eva might emphasize that retaining the vacation home allows Gabriel to preserve a family tradition, while other options balance financial stability for both parties.

Once you have put together the MESOs that reflect both your own and your ex's interests, you must be able to present them in a way that builds trust and collaboration rather than competition. One way to lay the groundwork for your presentation is to get prior agreement from your ex that you will be making the proposals. For example, Eva might say to Gabriel, "I've been thinking about some ways we might accomplish what matters most to both of us, and I wonder if you would be interested to hear some of my ideas at our next meeting. Would that work for you?"

Prior agreement helps reduce resistance and minimizes the risk of reactive devaluation (chapter 6), significantly increasing the likelihood that your ex will genuinely consider the proposals. This approach fosters an atmosphere of collaboration and respect, setting the stage for a productive discussion. By inviting your ex into the process and framing the proposals as part of a shared effort, you reduce defensiveness and open the door to constructive engagement.

WHILE MESOS OFFER a structured way to present multiple packages, it's also important to understand why packaging proposals—MESO or not—is such a powerful strategic tool in divorce negotiation.

Telling the Story

When issues are presented one at a time, negotiations can quickly devolve into a frustrating, tit-for-tat exchange. Each party becomes fixated on "winning" a single point, often leading to deadlock and entrenched positions.

Packaging proposals encourages a more holistic and flexible mindset. By combining related topics—such as child custody, spousal support, and asset division—you create the opportunity for meaningful trade-offs. Even when neither party gets everything they want on each point, a well-structured package can offer a resolution that feels balanced and fair overall.

However, to make these packages persuasive, you need to present them through a compelling narrative—one that connects the dots between logic, empathy, and shared values.

Storytelling is a powerful technique that connects with the other party on both an emotional and logical level. If you have listened to what your spouse values and paid attention without pushing back, you're in a strong position to create a narrative that resonates with their priorities and demonstrates your commitment to a mutually beneficial outcome.

What follows are some tips for crafting a narrative in your proposal.

Align With the Other Side's Interests

Make sure you understand the other party's priorities and reflect them in your proposal. For example, if your ex-spouse prioritizes stability for the children, your custody proposal might emphasize how your plan minimizes disruption to their routines—allowing them to stay in the same school, maintain relationships with their friends, and continue their extracurricular activities.

When you frame your proposal in terms of these priorities, you position yourself as a problem-solver rather than an adversary. This approach makes it easier for your spouse to accept your proposal as a reasonable and thoughtful solution.

Demonstrate Tactical Empathy

When one party holds more financial or emotional leverage—whether as the primary earner or the more dominant personality—tactical empathy (chapter 6) becomes an essential tool for leveling the playing field. Tactical empathy involves acknowledging the other party's concerns and perspectives, not as an agreement but as a demonstration of understanding.

For instance, if your spouse expresses anxiety about financial security, you might frame your asset division proposal in a way that highlights how it supports their goals while meeting your own. This acknowledgment of their concerns helps defuse defensiveness and fosters a cooperative tone.

Connect Emotionally

Great storytelling doesn't stop at logic—it taps into emotions. For example, when negotiating over a family home, you might frame your proposal by acknowledging its emotional significance and presenting a solution that preserves its value for the children.

Instead of a dry financial breakdown, you could say: "I know how much the kids love this house and how important it's been to all of us. My proposal allows them to stay here through the school year while we each transition into homes that reflect the next chapter of our lives." By weaving emotional resonance into your narrative, you create a proposal that feels thoughtful and responsive.

Increase Flexibility

Packaging proposals inherently provides greater flexibility. If the other party objects to one element of your proposal, you can adjust other parts of the package without derailing the entire negotiation. For instance, if your ex-spouse is hesitant about the division of retirement accounts, you might adjust the split of real estate assets or propose a different arrangement for spousal support as part of the overall package. This adaptability allows you to respond to their concerns while keeping the broader negotiation on track.

Reduce Impasse

When issues are addressed in isolation, it's easy to become stuck on a single point of contention. Packaging proposals avoids this pitfall by shifting the focus to the bigger picture. For example, rather than arguing over the exact value of one financial asset, you might frame the discussion as part of a comprehensive agreement that balances multiple concerns. This broader perspective reduces the likelihood of reaching an impasse and creates momentum that propels the negotiation forward.

Create Emotional Resonance in Packaging Proposals

In addition to the strategic benefits, packaged proposals can help address emotional dynamics. When you present a comprehensive solution, it signals thoughtfulness and a willingness to address the other party's needs holistically. This can build trust and reduce defensiveness, fostering a more collaborative environment.

For example, if one of your ex's primary concerns is stability for the children, a package that incorporates a consistent custody schedule alongside financial support for extracurricular activities demonstrates that you've listened to their priorities. By framing the proposal in a way that resonates emotionally, you create an opening for constructive dialogue.

Avoid Loss Framing

One common storytelling pitfall is focusing on what the other party might lose. Instead, reframe your proposal as a solution that offers benefits.

For example, instead of saying, "If you don't agree to this, you'll lose your share of the retirement account," reframe it as, "This proposal balances the financial security we both need for the future while allowing us to finalize things in a way that feels fair and forward-looking."

By focusing on gains rather than losses, you reduce the likelihood of resistance and promote a tone of collaboration.

SO YOU'VE presented your proposal packages in a timely manner and created a narrative of collaboration. However, the other party wants some concessions. How should you handle this?

Concessions: A Strategic Tool

Concessions aren't just a necessary part of negotiation—they're a powerful tool for building goodwill and maintaining momentum. Offering a well-planned concession signals your willingness to collaborate, creating a sense of reciprocity. When you give something up, the other party often feels obligated to do the same, helping you move closer to agreement. However, effective concessions require thoughtful planning. The goal is not to give in or appear weak but to strategically offer something that matters less to you in exchange for something more important. Here are some guidelines for effective concessions:

- **Know your priorities:** Clearly identify what you can trade and what you can't compromise on.

- **Be strategic:** Offer concessions that hold value for the other party but are less costly to you. For instance, Gabriel might offer a higher lump sum to Eva in exchange for keeping a sentimental property.

- **Frame positively:** Instead of saying "Fine, you can have it," express your flexibility as a thoughtful gesture: "I'm willing to adjust here because I want to find a solution that works for both of us."

- **Be mindful of timing:** Avoid making significant concessions too early, as doing this can set unrealistic expectations. Start with smaller concessions to gauge the response before offering larger ones when they have the most impact.

- **Link concessions to reciprocity:** Tie your concession to something you want in return. For example, Eva might say, "I'm open to reducing my share of the vacation home if we can agree on a larger share of retirement accounts."

Concessions should be purposeful, not impulsive. Even when you feel pressure to make a quick decision, take a moment to assess whether the trade-off aligns with your priorities. By managing concessions thoughtfully, you maintain credibility and avoid setting a pattern of over-giving.

Creating Trade-Offs

Bundling issues creates opportunities for meaningful trade-offs. For example, if you are negotiating both child custody and spousal

The goal is not to give in or appear weak but to strategically offer something that matters less to you in exchange for something more important.

support, you might propose a package that offers your ex a more favorable custody schedule in exchange for a higher support payment. This way, each party prioritizes what matters most to them while feeling that they've achieved a win.

Trade-offs also help build momentum. When one part of the package resonates with the other party's needs, they're more likely to view the entire proposal as constructive, which encourages collaboration.

When conventional approaches fail to yield results, and you find yourself stuck in a cycle of rigid positions or dismissive thinking, it may be time to use some creativity to break the deadlocks.

The Magic Theater

Borrowed from Hermann Hesse's novel *Steppenwolf*, the Magic Theater represents a place of limitless possibilities, imagination, and exploration beyond the constraints of ordinary reality. Stephen R. Covey discusses this concept in his book *The 3rd Alternative* as a powerful tool in negotiation for generating creative solutions that transcend the usual win-lose or compromise scenarios. The Magic Theater approach invites you to let go of judgment and preconceived notions temporarily. By doing so, you can explore ideas that might initially seem impractical or even impossible but that, with refinement, can lead to innovative and mutually satisfying outcomes.

For example, where divorce negotiations and proposals are concerned, instead of insisting on a fifty-fifty division, you could explore creative ways to allocate assets that prioritize individual preferences and values. Perhaps one party keeps a family-owned business while the other retains the primary residence, or one party takes more liquid assets while the other receives a larger share of long-term investments. Or if one party values stability for the children while the other is concerned about financial security, the Magic Theater approach might inspire the creation of a trust fund for the children's education. Such a trust could ensure stability for the kids while offering tax benefits and financial planning advantages for the contributing spouse. These kinds of creative solutions can address the emotional and practical needs of both parties in ways that standard negotiation tactics might overlook.

The Magic Theater is not just about brainstorming individually—it's about creating a shared space where both parties can collaborate on solutions that go beyond their initial perspectives. If you want to use the Magic Theater to stimulate creative thinking, you'll need to do the following:

- **Suspend your judgment:** Temporarily set aside practical limitations and allow yourself to think beyond the ordinary.
- **Focus on interests:** Keep both parties' core interests at the forefront while brainstorming.
- **Invite collaboration:** Encourage your ex-spouse to join in the process by framing it as an opportunity to co-create solutions.
- **Refine and adapt:** Once you've explored creative ideas, work together to adapt them into practical proposals.

This shared problem-solving approach reduces defensiveness and builds goodwill, making it easier to reach an agreement that both parties feel good about. This fosters a sense of partnership, even in the midst of a negotiation, and helps reframe the process as a joint effort to build a better future.

The Third Alternative

Covey also showcases the "Third Alternative" approach as a way to move beyond traditional negotiation outcomes—such as compromise or concession—toward a solution that transcends the limitations of either party's initial position. The Third Alternative is not just a middle ground, but a creative synthesis that produces a better outcome than either party could achieve on their own.

Unlike a traditional win-win approach, where each party makes concessions to reach mutual agreement, Covey's Third Alternative emphasizes solutions where *everyone* benefits—not just the two primary negotiators but also others affected by the outcome, like children in a divorce.

The Third Alternative seeks to maximize gains for all involved. For instance, if a divorcing couple is negotiating child custody, the goal isn't just to split time evenly (a win-win). Instead, they could create a shared parenting plan that not only ensures equal time but also incorporates special activities, shared traditions, or even creative living arrangements that enhance the children's emotional and developmental needs. In this way, the children become the "third win," benefiting from their parents' collaborative efforts.

Imagine Eva and Gabriel are stuck on how to divide time with their children. Gabriel wants a predictable schedule to accommodate his creative work, while Eva values flexibility for her entrepreneurial pursuits. Instead of settling for a rigid split, they might use the Third Alternative approach to design a dynamic schedule that adapts as their careers and children's needs evolve. They could also include shared experiences like family dinners or celebrations that maintain continuity for their children and foster goodwill between the parents.

The Third Alternative relies on the principle of synergy: the idea that the whole is greater than the sum of its parts. So Covey suggests starting with a powerful reframing question: "What is a solution that is better than what either of us could come up with alone?" inviting both parties to shift their mindset from competition to collaboration. For instance, in dividing financial assets, one party may prioritize liquidity while the other values stability. A synergistic solution might involve allocating liquid assets to one party for immediate needs while creating long-term investments for the other. Alternatively, the couple could agree on creative arrangements like shared ownership of income-generating assets (such as rental properties) to ensure both parties benefit from future growth.

Pursuing a Third Alternative can positively transform the emotional tone of a negotiation while, practically speaking, fostering resilience. As an added benefit, co-created solutions are less likely to unravel under future stress because they reflect shared ownership and alignment with both parties' long-term interests.

Applying the Magic Theater and Third Alternative Approaches

Negotiations often stall when both parties focus on their fixed positions instead of exploring deeper interests or creative possibilities. The Magic Theater and the Third Alternative encourage open-mindedness, collaboration, and innovation—helping you move beyond routine problem-solving to discover new paths for agreement. Here are key steps to help you apply these transformative methods:

- **Set the stage for creativity:** Temporarily suspend your assumptions about what's "realistic" or "acceptable" and invite the other person to brainstorm freely. If you're stuck dividing assets, for example, explore unconventional ideas such as shared ownership or staggered payouts to accommodate each party's specific needs.

- **Pose the Third Alternative question:** Ask, "What is a solution that's better than what either of us could come up with alone?" By reframing the problem this way, you shift from competing to collaborating. For instance, if you and your ex are at odds over custody arrangements, this question might prompt schedules that adapt to your children's changing needs or include shared family activities.

- **Brainstorm without judgment:** Write down all ideas—no matter how impractical—before critiquing them. This free-flow process often leads to unexpected combinations. If one spouse values financial stability while the other values emotional continuity for the children, you might create a joint trust fund that meets both goals.

- **Combine and refine ideas:** Look for ways to adjust promising suggestions or merge them into a more cohesive plan. If you both want to keep the family home but neither of you can afford it alone, consider joint ownership with a buyout option after a set period. Or agree to sell the property and allocate the proceeds toward separate living arrangements that fit each person's needs.

- **Test and adjust:** Compare your emerging solution against each party's BATNA and WATNA (Best and Worst Alternatives to a Negotiated Agreement). If a custody schedule seems ideal but doesn't work with a child's extracurriculars, adjust accordingly so it still honors both parents' roles.

- **Present as a package:** Rather than offering isolated fixes—like discussing only asset division or only custody—bundle your ideas into a comprehensive agreement. Showing how one issue's resolution complements that of another can reduce the chance of deadlock and encourage a sense of shared progress.

By following these steps, you expand your negotiation tool kit beyond simple compromise, opening the door to genuinely creative solutions that address the core concerns of everyone involved.

These two creative approaches to breaking impasses in negotiation work because they focus on possibility rather than limitation. The Magic Theater encourages you to think beyond conventional boundaries, while the Third Alternative emphasizes creating something better than compromise. Together, they allow you to approach negotiations with a mindset of abundance, turning challenges into opportunities for growth and resolution.

AS YOU refine your approach to proposals—whether through MESOS or creative techniques like the Magic Theater—you'll naturally encounter moments of friction. The next chapter shows you how to navigate conflict effectively so you can maintain a constructive atmosphere even when disagreements surface. By learning how to address tension head-on, you'll stay on course toward a resolution that meets everyone's interests.

KEY TAKEAWAYS

- **Anchor your proposals:** Begin with a well-timed, fair anchor that sets a reference point and frames the negotiation in your favor.

- **Package issues strategically:** Bundle multiple topics together to create trade-offs, reduce impasses, and foster a holistic approach.

- **Use MESOs for flexibility:** Present multiple equivalent offers to empower your spouse, minimize resistance, and encourage collaborative problem-solving.

- **Make use of storytelling:** Craft proposals with empathetic narratives that align with both parties' interests and emotional needs.

- **Plan concessions wisely:** Offer targeted, well-prepared concessions tied to reciprocal gains to build goodwill and maintain momentum.

- **Seek creative approaches when deadlocked:** Use techniques like the Magic Theater or the Third Alternative to suspend judgments, explore new ideas, and co-create solutions that go beyond concessions and compromise for truly beneficial outcomes.

10

Navigating Conflict in Negotiation

ONFLICT IS an inevitable part of divorce negotiations, but it doesn't have to derail the process—or be unhealthy. At its core, conflict is deeply tied to the emotions of divorce—anger, fear, grief, and even guilt—all of which can intensify and perpetuate disputes. Even for those who have worked through their emotions, the negotiation process itself often brings those feelings roaring back to the surface. This is especially true when critical decisions about children, finances, or the future feel deeply personal or unfair. But not all conflict stems from emotional reactivity. Sometimes, it's simply a reflection of differing interests, expectations, values, or opinions. When explored thoughtfully, those differences can lead to more creative, durable outcomes for everyone involved.

This chapter bridges the gap between understanding the emotions of divorce and using that understanding to navigate and manage conflict in negotiation. While conflicts can feel overwhelming during this critical phase, the insights and tools I'll offer here should help you shift from unproductive, emotional cycles of conflict to more constructive dialogue, paving the way for understanding, growth, and, where possible, resolution.

In particular, we'll revisit the *conflict trap* (chapter 2), a cycle of escalating reactions that keeps negotiations stuck in patterns of retaliation. And we'll look closely at *conflict dynamics*, the underlying forces—like power imbalances, communication styles, and emotional triggers—that shape how disputes unfold. These concepts are more than theoretical; they provide a practical lens for understanding and managing conflict in real time even when the stakes feel impossibly high.

Breaking Free from the Conflict Trap

The conflict trap refers to a pattern of behavior where initial conflicts lead to a series of reactions and counterreactions, causing the conflict to escalate rather than being resolved. Once people are caught in this trap, it becomes difficult to break free. Each new round of conflict reinforces previous grievances and leads to further entrenchment of people's positions and a deepening of their dispute.

Married for fifteen years, Portia and Rodney had developed distinct conflict styles that often clashed. Portia tended to be more confrontational, addressing issues head-on and insisting on discussing problems until they were resolved. Rodney, on the other hand, preferred to avoid conflict, often shutting down or withdrawing when tensions arose. Over the years, this dynamic led to unresolved issues festering beneath the surface, leaving both partners feeling unheard and misunderstood.

Now, as they faced divorce, these long-standing conflict styles and unresolved issues resurfaced with new intensity. The division of the family home became a flashpoint that quickly escalated into a full-blown conflict trap. Here's how that unfolded for Portia and Rodney.

- **First retaliation:** Portia, drawing from her direct conflict style, pushed hard for her position on the house, framing it as essential for the children's well-being. Rodney, feeling cornered and dismissed, retaliated by demanding full custody of the children.

- **Counter-retaliation:** Portia, feeling that Rodney's demand for full custody was an extreme overreaction and an attack on her role as a mother, responded with even more intensity. She brought up past grievances, such as Rodney's perceived emotional absence during their marriage, and accused him of using the children to get back at her. Rodney, uncomfortable with the confrontation and feeling unfairly attacked, withdrew further, but this time with a resolve to "stand his ground," exacerbating the conflict.

- **Entrenchment:** Both Portia and Rodney became entrenched in their positions. Portia refused to consider any compromise, insisting she was fighting for the children's best interests. Rodney, feeling increasingly alienated, became equally rigid, refusing to negotiate on the house or custody.

Portia and Rodney's escalating conflict wasn't just about the house or custody. Unresolved marital grievances and conflict styles were preventing them from recognizing that their current conflict was shaped as much by the past as by the present. Although often well-meaning, Portia's direct approach came across as forceful and aggressive to Rodney. Her insistence on resolving issues immediately often escalated the situation, particularly with someone like Rodney who preferred to avoid confrontation. But Rodney's preference to shut down or retreat in the face of conflict left Portia feeling dismissed and unheard. And his avoidance often manifested in indirect retaliation, like withholding documents or making unreasonable demands, which only deepened Portia's frustration.

Recognizing this pattern was the first step to breaking free.

As their mediator, I encouraged Portia and Rodney to reflect on how their conflict styles and unresolved history were influencing the current negotiation. I helped them see that their reactions were more about unresolved conflicts and unmet needs from their marriage. I suggested they pause and consider alternative ways to communicate their needs: Portia by softening her approach to make room for dialogue, and Rodney by engaging more actively rather than withdrawing. We discussed shifting the focus from past grievances to creative solutions that addressed both of their underlying concerns.

For instance, we explored ways to approach the house and custody as a package (chapter 9) rather than separate issues, allowing for more collaborative solutions. I also recommended involving a child psychologist to help determine what was truly in the children's best interests, shifting the focus away from their personal grievances.

Empowering Yourself by Taking Responsibility
Breaking the conflict trap often begins with taking responsibility for your own role in the dynamic. While it's tempting to focus on the other person's flaws, true empowerment comes from changing what you can control: your own responses. If you change the way you are responding in the conversation, you are likely to get a different reaction than the one you have always gotten, and that can free you from the conflict trap.

Like many of us, I've had moments where my own defensive reactions have escalated conflicts in my life. For example, if my husband points out that he's been the one unloading the dishwasher for two weeks and suggests I take it over tomorrow, my natural instinct is to snap back about the recycling not being taken out. But when I take a breath and pause, I can see what's really happening. I realize that snapping back won't make me feel better, nor will it make him feel heard. Instead, I can acknowledge what he's saying without defensiveness. That shift in how I respond changes the tone of the conversation entirely.

This same principle applies to Portia and Rodney. By acknowledging their own roles in the dynamic and making small adjustments—Portia softening her approach and Rodney staying engaged—they were able to break free from the trap and move toward a resolution that worked for everyone.

Conflict Dynamics

Conflict dynamics refer to the underlying forces and patterns that drive and shape conflict over time. Understanding these dynamics can help you anticipate how conflicts might evolve and what factors could either exacerbate or mitigate the conflict. When you're aware of these dynamics, you can shift your perspective from reacting emotionally to responding strategically in your divorce negotiation. What follows are the key elements of conflict dynamics to consider.

Trigger Events

Conflicts often have specific trigger events that set them in motion. These triggers can be external, such as filing for divorce or a disagreement over parenting schedules, or internal, like a misunderstanding or miscommunication.

For example, in Portia and Rodney's negotiation, the trigger event was Portia's statement about the children needing to stay in the family home. While her intention was to prioritize the children's well-being, Rodney interpreted her words as dismissive of his financial contributions. This simple miscommunication became the spark that reignited years of tension.

By identifying the triggers in your own conflicts, you can better understand the root causes and prevent unnecessary escalation.

Power Imbalances

Power dynamics play a significant role in how conflicts unfold. In negotiations, perceived or actual power imbalances can lead to one party dominating the conversation, which breeds resentment and resistance in the other party. In divorce, these imbalances often arise from disparities in financial resources, legal knowledge, or decision-making authority during the marriage.

For instance, if one spouse controls the finances, they might use this advantage to pressure the other spouse during negotiations. This perceived imbalance can make the other party feel disempowered and lead to defensiveness or retaliation. Addressing power imbalances—through education, advocacy, or the support of a neutral mediator—can create a more equitable dynamic and reduce the potential for escalation.

While it's tempting to focus
on the other person's flaws,
true empowerment comes from
changing what you can control:
your own responses.

Communication Patterns

The way each party communicates during a conflict can either fuel or defuse the situation. Open, respectful communication between them promotes understanding, while aggressive or passive communication often exacerbates tensions. Consider how the communication patterns played a role for Portia and Rodney. Their contrasting styles created a feedback loop of frustration. Recognizing your own communication tendencies can help you adapt and create space for constructive dialogue.

Emotional Reactions

Emotions such as anger, fear, and hurt often drive conflict dynamics. These emotions can cloud judgment, lead to impulsive decisions, and fuel misinterpretations of the other party's actions.

In heated moments, emotions can take over. For Rodney, the fear of being sidelined in decisions about the children led to an emotional reaction—his sudden demand for full custody. This escalated the conflict, leaving Portia feeling attacked and retaliating with accusations about his past behavior.

Managing emotional responses is essential to navigating conflict effectively. By pausing and acknowledging your emotions, you can regain control and respond with clarity rather than impulsivity.

Conflict Spirals

Conflicts can spiral when negative behaviors and attitudes feed off each other. For example, if one party responds to a perceived slight with hostility, the other party may escalate the hostility in return, creating a feedback loop that deepens the conflict.

Portia and Rodney's conflict spiraled when Rodney withheld financial documents after feeling dismissed and Portia retaliated with harsh accusations. Each action fueled the other, making resolution seem impossible.

Breaking a conflict spiral requires intentional effort to pause, reset, and redirect the dynamic.

Managing Conflict Dynamics

Although understanding conflict dynamics is important, the next step is learning how to manage them effectively. Here are some practical strategies you can use.

- **Anticipate reactions:** Try to anticipate how the other party might react to certain actions or proposals. By understanding their likely responses, you can tailor your approach to avoid unnecessary escalation.

- **Promote positive interaction:** Encourage positive, solution-oriented communication. This might involve acknowledging the other party's concerns, offering genuine concessions, or reframing the conflict in a way that highlights shared interests. For example, instead of framing a parenting proposal as "I need the kids to stay with me," you might say, "I think the kids would benefit from consistency right now—how can we work together to create that?"

- **Focus on interests, not positions:** Shifting the focus from rigid positions to underlying interests can transform a conflict from adversarial to collaborative. For example, instead of insisting on a specific financial settlement, explore how different options can meet both parties' financial security needs.

- **Use de-escalation techniques:** Such techniques as active listening, empathy, and taking breaks when discussions become heated can help calm the situation and prevent the conflict from spiraling out of control.

- **Third-party mediation:** Sometimes, bringing in a neutral third party, such as a mediator, can provide an objective perspective and facilitate constructive communication. A skilled mediator can help balance power dynamics, keep the focus on interests, and guide both parties toward resolution. I'll talk more about this later in the chapter.

When you recognize the patterns that can lead to escalation and employ strategies to manage and resolve conflicts constructively, you can avoid getting trapped in cycles of retaliation and work toward solutions that benefit both parties.

However, if you find yourself stuck in a negotiation, take a step back. Ask yourself: Has the conflict trap caught me? What can I do to interrupt the cycle and reach a different result? Those insights aren't just about resolving divorce negotiations—they're about empowering yourself to approach conflict in a way that fosters understanding, collaboration, and meaningful solutions.

Understanding conflict dynamics is essential for navigating disputes effectively. But when these dynamics intersect with significant power imbalances, negotiations can become especially challenging and even intimidating.

Dealing With Bullies

Many individuals who dominate or control negotiations may not recognize their own behavior, especially if they are accustomed to high-stakes decision-making in their professional lives. This dynamic can leave their spouses feeling powerless, unheard, or unable to advocate effectively for themselves, particularly when there is an imbalance in confidence, expertise, or resources.

The American Psychological Association defines bullying as "persistent threatening and aggressive physical behavior or verbal abuse directed toward other people, especially those who are younger, smaller, weaker, or in some way more vulnerable than the bully." This definition highlights three critical elements pertinent to divorce proceedings:

1 The behavior is intended to harm or disturb.
2 It occurs repeatedly over time.
3 There is an imbalance of power, with a more powerful person or group exerting control over a less powerful one.

In the context of negotiation, bullying often manifests as verbal or psychological intimidation. This might include dismissive remarks, leveraging expertise to overwhelm the other party, or financial manipulation. The essence of bullying lies in the use of intimidation to dominate the process, leaving the less powerful party feeling overwhelmed and helpless.

I often hear from individuals who worry about facing a spouse in negotiations—especially one who is experienced in hard-driving tactics. Their concern is often rooted in feeling disadvantaged or overwhelmed by the imbalance of power. To illustrate how power imbalances and bullying can manifest in negotiations, consider the following scenarios:

- The Successful Entrepreneur: Imagine a husband who is a successful entrepreneur known for his aggressive negotiation tactics in business. In marriage, this same approach often left his wife feeling unheard and overwhelmed. During their divorce negotiations, he dominates conversations, interrupting and dismissing her concerns about child custody arrangements. He uses his financial acumen and knowledge of legal loopholes to pressure her into accepting a less favorable settlement—one that serves his needs while disregarding hers.

- The Financial Expert: In another case, a husband is a financial expert who has always managed the family's finances. During negotiations, he uses his superior knowledge of their financial situation to intimidate his wife, suggesting she wouldn't understand the complexities involved in dividing assets fairly. He throws around financial jargon or presents skewed figures to convince her that his proposal is the best she can get, leaving her feeling powerless and unsure of how to advocate for herself.

- The Overbearing Professional: Consider a husband married to a high-powered attorney accustomed to winning arguments. In mediation, she uses her legal expertise and forceful personality to steamroll him, dismissing his concerns about asset division or alimony. Without legal representation of his own, he feels pressured to agree to terms that are not in his best interest, simply because he cannot match her legal knowledge or confidence.

In the examples above, the perceived power imbalance creates a dynamic where one party feels disadvantaged, making it difficult to engage in fair and productive negotiations. Without intervention, this can lead to a skewed and unjust outcome. In such situations, attorneys can level the playing field by providing the necessary support and advocacy to ensure the less powerful party's voice is heard and that the negotiation remains balanced and fair.

If you're facing a bully in negotiation, here are steps you can take to protect yourself and ensure the process remains fair:

- **Recognize the dynamics:** Understanding when bullying or intimidation is at play is the first step. Pay attention to patterns of dominance, manipulation, or dismissal.

- **Seek support:** Don't face the negotiation alone. Whether it's attorneys, a mediator, a financial advisor, or another trusted professional, having a support team can help balance the power dynamic.

- **Stand your ground:** While it's important to remain calm, don't hesitate to assert your needs and interests clearly. Bullies often back down when they encounter firm and consistent boundaries.

- **Leverage neutral mediators:** A skilled mediator can help manage power imbalances by facilitating equal participation and keeping the focus on constructive dialogue.

- **Document everything:** Keep detailed records of interactions, proposals, and decisions. Documentation provides clarity and ensures you have a record in case disputes arise later.

When bullying or significant power imbalances are present, it's pivotal that you understand the conflict dynamics at play. By recognizing these dynamics early, you can take the necessary steps to ensure that negotiations are conducted fairly and that both parties have an equal opportunity to participate. David Emerald's *The Power of TED** offers a helpful lens here: instead of staying stuck in the roles of victim, persecutor, or rescuer, you can begin to shift into more constructive roles—creator, challenger, and coach. This reframing doesn't minimize the presence of power dynamics, but it empowers you to respond with clarity and intention rather than reactivity.

In cases where bullying or intimidation is present, involving legal or professional support can make all the difference. It not only protects the interests of the less powerful party but also helps facilitate a more equitable and constructive outcome. If you find yourself in a negotiation with someone who dominates or intimidates, remind yourself: You are not powerless. With the right tools, support, and mindset, you can navigate even the most challenging dynamics and advocate for a fair resolution.

Bullying isn't always easy to recognize in others, let alone in ourselves. Often, when we feel wronged or frustrated, we may resort to behaviors that, while unintended, come across as controlling or intimidating to the other person. A desire to be heard or to make the other person "see reason" can sometimes push us into unproductive patterns of behavior.

Ryan and Nora: A Case of Misaligned Perspectives

Ryan came to me several years ago for help with his divorce. Financial disagreements had been a constant source of tension in his marriage with Nora. Ryan believed she used bullying tactics when it came to money. Whenever he tried to address the family's overspending, she would justify her actions by saying the spending was "for the kids." She would also insist that cutting back their expenses would hurt the children and damage their relationship with him.

After I was retained, I followed my usual practice of reaching out to Nora's lawyer to get a sense of the issues at hand and how we might resolve them. During our conversation, Nora's lawyer shared that Nora felt bullied by Ryan. She described him as "always trying to control her spending and guilting her for spending too much." Nora's lawyer reiterated Nora's comment that her spending was "for the kids" and suggested Ryan needed to back off his overly critical and controlling behavior.

When I recounted this conversation to Ryan, he was stunned. To him, he was simply being responsible and trying to get Nora to understand how certain purchases—like expensive clothing for their daughter—were preventing them from saving for college. Ryan explained that his repeated attempts to get through to Nora often escalated into frustration, and he admitted that he sometimes raised his voice as he became more insistent. He believed Nora's spending was reckless and thoughtless; especially given the financial pressure he felt as the primary wage earner.

Then I asked Ryan a simple question: "Do you think Nora is trying to put pressure on you?"

He paused, clearly taken aback. After thinking for a moment, he responded, "No, I think Nora wants our daughter to feel like she fits in with her classmates, even though her parents are divorcing." This moment of reflection was transformative. As Ryan considered Nora's actions through a new lens, his frustration began to soften. He realized that her spending wasn't an intentional effort to create conflict; it was an attempt to protect their daughter's emotional well-being during a turbulent time.

I watched Ryan's expression change as he took a deep breath. The realization that Nora's behavior wasn't malicious allowed him to approach the negotiation with a new perspective. Instead of framing the discussion as a battle over right and wrong, we shifted the focus to a conversation about choices and the allocation of resources.

Ryan's story is a powerful reminder that feeling justified in our frustration doesn't absolve us from the impact of our actions. Even when we feel wronged, it's possible to unintentionally adopt behaviors that come across as controlling, dismissive, or even bullying. Here are some signs to watch for in yourself:

- **Repeated insistence on being "right"**: Are you trying to "win" the conversation instead of seeking understanding?
- **Escalating volume or intensity**: Are you raising your voice or becoming more insistent when you don't feel heard?
- **Being dismissive**: Are you viewing the other person's actions as unreasonable or dismissing their perspective without considering their underlying motivations?

If you recognize these patterns in yourself, take a moment to pause and reflect. Ask yourself:

- **What am I trying to achieve?** Are you focused on resolution, or are you stuck in proving your point?
- **What might the other person be feeling or needing?** Shifting your perspective to consider their motivations can reveal common ground.
- **How can I reframe the conversation?** Move from a right-versus-wrong mindset to a collaborative one focused on finding solutions that work for both parties. Ask yourself, Why am I having this reaction? What is really going on here?

For Ryan, this shift in thinking opened the door to a more productive and empathetic negotiation. By reframing Nora's spending as an effort to support their daughter, rather than an act of defiance or irresponsibility, he was able to approach the discussion with curiosity and openness.

When you take the time to reflect on your own behavior, you not only gain greater insight into the dynamics at play, you also empower yourself to change the tone of the conversation and work toward a resolution that honors the needs of everyone involved.

The Power of Neutrality

Navigating the challenging waters of negotiation—especially when power imbalances or bullying behaviors are present—can feel daunting. However, there's a powerful tool that can break through these barriers and create a space for true dialogue and resolution. During the years I have worked as a mediator, I've witnessed countless stories of conflict and resolution and learned some surprising truths. Perhaps the most remarkable discovery is the transformative power of neutrality in conflict resolution.

People embroiled in conflict—particularly conflicts intense enough to involve legal intervention—often believe they can't agree

When you take the time to reflect on your own behavior, you not only gain greater insight into the dynamics at play, you also empower yourself to change the tone of the conversation.

on anything. This belief creates a rigid mindset where each party feels that any concession, even on minor points, signals weakness or vulnerability.

For instance, in divorce negotiations, a spouse might say something like, "He's a good dad, but he's never home." On the surface, this seems like a balanced acknowledgment. In reality, it couples praise with criticism, undermining any potential agreement. This pattern of thinking—where agreeing on anything feels like conceding too much—occurs in virtually every conflict.

Whether in divorce, business disputes, or other contentious situations, parties often become so entrenched in their positions that they lose sight of areas where they might agree. This is where neutrality and the role of a neutral mediator become essential.

The Role of a Neutral Mediator

A neutral mediator plays a pivotal role in helping people in divorce negotiations recognize and break emotional and behavioral patterns that are preventing them from finding common ground. When parties agree to work with a mediator, they unknowingly take two significant steps toward resolution:

1 **They are agreeing to resolve the conflict:** Choosing mediation demonstrates that both parties, despite their differences, want to resolve the conflict. This step may seem obvious, but it represents a crucial willingness to move beyond the impasse.

2 **They are sharing trust in the process:** Selecting a neutral third party signifies shared trust in the process, even if the parties don't fully trust each other. The mediator's neutrality provides a safe space for both parties to express concerns and work toward solutions without fear of bias or favoritism.

These agreements form a powerful covenant between the parties. This covenant represents common ground—a small but significant foundation of trust and cooperation that can feel almost magical compared to the hostility often present in conflict. The skillful mediator uses neutrality to build on this initial foundation and foster further agreements. Here's how neutrality works its magic.

- **Building trust:** A neutral mediator helps build trust by creating an environment where both parties feel safe expressing their true concerns and needs. Without the fear of favoritism, parties are more likely to engage openly and honestly.
- **Focusing on common goals:** The mediator helps the parties focus on shared goals rather than their differences. For example, in a divorce, both parents may want to ensure their children's well-being. By keeping the focus on shared objectives, the mediator facilitates solutions that work for both parties.
- **Encouraging honest dialogue:** Because the mediator is neutral, they can encourage honest and respectful dialogue. This de-escalates tensions, allowing both parties to feel heard and understood, which paves the way for constructive discussions.
- **Creating momentum:** Each small agreement reached—whether it's on the process, the mediator, or a minor issue—builds momentum toward resolution. These incremental steps build confidence in the process and make further agreements easier to achieve.

In situations where power imbalances or bullying behaviors are present, neutrality can be a game-changer. It creates a space where both parties feel valued and heard, reducing the likelihood of one party dominating the negotiation. But the true magic of neutrality isn't just about resolving one conflict—it's about transforming how people in conflict view each other and the situation. By engaging with a neutral mediator, even the most entrenched disputes can shift from hostility to collaboration. Neutrality makes the seemingly impossible becomes possible. Even in the most contentious negotiations, neutrality creates the conditions for meaningful dialogue, collaboration, and, ultimately, resolution.

But sometimes there can come a point when everything feels hopeless.

When Things Seem Impossible

In any negotiation, particularly those involving deeply entrenched conflicts, at some point parties may find themselves locked into their respective views, seemingly unwilling or unable to move. At this juncture, fear often takes hold, creating a palpable tension in the room that drives people further apart.

When faced with such situations, lawyers and other professionals often react in one of two ways: either by pushing harder toward settlement—sometimes resorting to scare tactics—or by giving up, declaring the situation an impasse.

I don't like the word *impasse*—it suggests that the difficulty you are facing is as solid and unyielding as concrete, an immovable barrier that cannot be overcome. Furthermore, we don't have a special word for a negotiation that's flowing smoothly, where everyone is engaged and making progress toward a mutually beneficial solution. Why, then, should we dignify moments of stuckness with a word that implies permanence and futility?

The truth is, difficult moments are a natural part of the negotiation process. Sometimes things do seem impossible, and that's to be expected. But when this happens, it's not a cause for panic. Instead, it's an opportunity—an invitation to reassess, to pause, and to explore new ways forward. When the negotiation feels stuck, there are several strategies that can help return the process to a state of flow—none of which requires one side to simply capitulate.

Take a Step Back

Sometimes the way the discussions are structured is the root of the problem. Perhaps the wrong people are in the room or the focus is on the wrong area of the conflict. Participants might lack the information they need to make informed decisions, or emotions may be running too high to engage productively. Taking a step back to examine what's working—and what isn't—can help get the conversation back on track.

For example, imagine a divorce negotiation where the parents are stuck on deciding who should keep the family home. Financial advisors dominate the conversation, but neither parent feels *emotionally* ready to let go of the home due to its significance to their children. Bringing in a child psychologist or family therapist to focus on the emotional well-being of the children could shift the perspective, offering new solutions. Perhaps joint ownership of the home until the children graduate from high school becomes a possibility—one that aligns with both parents' values and goals.

In another case, a couple was negotiating the division of a family business. The wife, who had built the business from the ground up, was deeply attached to it, while the husband saw it primarily as a financial asset. The discussions became increasingly tense, with both parties feeling stuck and defensive. Realizing that the conversation was going in circles, the mediator suggested taking a step back and pausing negotiations for a few days. During this time, both parties had space to reflect on their positions.

When they reconvened, the wife acknowledged that her resistance stemmed from a fear of losing her identity and sense of purpose, while the husband, though still focused on financial outcomes, recognized that pushing for a quick sale might not only escalate conflict but devalue the business. This new awareness allowed them to explore creative solutions, such as a phased buyout that gave the wife time to transition out while still securing financial stability for both.

Explore Motivation to Stay in the Negotiation

It can be helpful to examine why each party is motivated to continue—or leave—the negotiation. What do they hope to achieve? Are they bogged down by trivial matters that obscure the core issues? For example, a negotiation over spousal support might become sidetracked by arguments over minor household items or old grievances.

These distractions could be masking deeper concerns about financial stability or future security. Refocusing the discussion on long-term financial planning, perhaps with the help of a financial planner, can shift the conversation back to what truly matters and help the parties find common ground.

Breathing Into the Impossibility

In his guided meditations, Norman Fischer (founder of the Everyday Zen Foundation) often suggests the practice of "breathing into" a problem or discomfort to see what happens. This concept can be applied to negotiations as well. Instead of reacting to the sense of impossibility with panic or aggression, consider breathing into the situation—both figuratively and literally. That means noticing the discomfort, pausing to take a breath, and creating space before reacting. Rather than rushing to fix or avoid the tension, allow yourself and the other parties to sit with it. Often, clarity emerges not from forcing a solution but from tolerating uncertainty long enough to hear what really matters.

For example, in a heated divorce negotiation over the division of retirement assets, both spouses might feel entitled to the larger share, leading to an emotional standoff. Instead of pushing forward with arguments, the mediator might suggest taking a break and encouraging each party to reflect on their future needs and goals. When they reconvene, one spouse proposes reallocating other assets—such as real estate or personal property—to balance the division of retirement funds. This new perspective opens the door to further discussion and leads to a more balanced agreement.

AS YOU close this chapter, reflect on how mastering conflict dynamics has equipped you to break free from destructive cycles. These insights don't just resolve disputes; they lay the groundwork for making wiser, more intentional decisions. Now, having navigated the storm of emotions and entrenched behaviors, your focus shifts from managing conflict to evaluating outcomes. In the final chapter, I'll explore how to manage your emotions (and your lawyer) during the final stages to make sure that the agreements you reach not only resolve your disputes but pave the way for a stable, empowered future.

KEY TAKEAWAYS

- **Recognize the conflict trap:** Unresolved grievances can escalate quickly. Taking responsibility for your role helps defuse tension.

- **Identify conflict dynamics:** Triggers, power imbalances, and emotional spirals often fuel disputes. Awareness lets you respond strategically rather than reactively.

- **Beware of bullying:** Intimidation undermines fairness. Seek support, stand firm on your needs, and use mediators or attorneys to address power imbalances.

- **Embrace neutrality:** A skilled mediator fosters trust, highlights shared goals, and can encourage people in entrenched positions toward collaboration.

- **Overcome "impossible" moments:** To restore momentum and find solutions, you can step back to reevaluate negotiation structure, allow everyone enough time to process, and focus on genuine motivations.

11

The Final Stages: Is This the Right Deal?

MARCY SAT AT the dining room table, staring at the papers before her. Negotiations with Steve had dragged on for months, leaving her feeling trapped. She had chosen collaborative divorce, believing it was the best option for maintaining dignity and respect, but that didn't ease the process. Clarity about her future still felt distant.

The house was the sticking point. Marcy wanted to stay in the home where Harrison and Emma had grown up—a place steeped in memories. To her, it symbolized stability during such an uncertain time. However, Steve was reluctant to support her staying for more than two years. His practical reasons clashed with Marcy's emotional needs. She wanted to remain until the children graduated high school, ensuring continuity in their lives. However, the support Steve offered wasn't enough to carry the house and sustain their current lifestyle. Staying would mean constant financial stress and cutting back on what made the house feel like home.

Every option felt like a loss to Marcy. If she stayed, she'd worry endlessly about money. If she moved, she feared losing the security the house represented for her children. Some days, she considered giving in—agreeing to whatever Steve wanted just to end the uncertainty. Other days, she was tempted to walk away from the process entirely and take her chances in court.

One sleepless night, lying in bed, Marcy's thoughts turned to Harrison and Emma. She wanted to protect them from the fallout of the divorce, but the weight of her decisions felt crushing. She was angry at Steve for putting them in this position and at herself for not seeing it coming. Beneath the anger was an overwhelming sense of loss. Every decision felt like another step away from the life she had envisioned for her family.

Then, something shifted. Marcy realized she had been so focused on what she was losing that she hadn't considered what she might gain. Staying in the house might provide stability, but it also tethered her to a past life that no longer existed. Moving, while painful, could be an opportunity—a chance to build a new life for herself and her children, free from the shadows of what was.

The next morning, she called me. I could hear the shift in her voice.

"I've been thinking about the house," she said, her tone steadier than it had been in weeks. "For so long, I thought staying was the only way to keep things stable for Harrison and Emma. But maybe it's not. Maybe it's time to look at other options."

"That's a big realization, Marcy," I said gently. "Letting go of the house doesn't mean letting go of stability for your kids. It just means finding a new way to provide it. If you're open to it, we can use the house as a starting point to negotiate for what really matters."

Marcy took a deep breath. "I think I'm ready to do that. But I need to ensure we get something in return—something that provides real security for me and the kids."

"We can absolutely do that," I assured her. "We'll focus on negotiating additional support or assets that give you the flexibility to create a new home and life. There may also be other non-financial concessions we can explore."

By the end of our conversation, Marcy's resolve was clear. She wasn't giving up the house out of defeat; she was choosing to let go of what no longer served her to make room for something new.

As I reflected on our call, I felt confident that Marcy was in a much stronger position. She was approaching the negotiations with clarity, focusing on long-term goals rather than short-term fears. This mindset shift was key—not just for the negotiations, but for the life she was building for herself and her children.

The Importance of Mindset in Final Negotiations

As you approach the final stages of your divorce negotiation, your mindset becomes crucial. Likely the process has been long and emotionally taxing, but these final decisions will shape your future and how you approach them matters a lot. Like Marcy, your priorities may have shifted over time; now is the moment to reassess them. Are your initial goals still aligned with your long-term vision?

When I went through my divorce, I was determined to keep my home, an apartment on the Upper West Side of Manhattan. At the time, it felt essential for maintaining stability for myself and my children. However, after the divorce was finalized, I visited my ex-husband's new apartment—smaller, more manageable, and less stressful financially and physically. Standing there, I thought, "I should have moved somewhere like this." It was a wake-up call that clinging to my original ideas about what was best for me and my children might not have been the most strategic choice. This realization has shaped how I guide my clients through the final stages of negotiation.

Amy Edmondson, a prominent researcher on organizational behavior, discusses psychological safety in her book *The Fearless Organization: Creating Psychological Safety in the Workplace for Learning, Innovation, and Growth*. Edmondson emphasizes how fear can inhibit our ability to think clearly and perform at our best. This concept applies to divorce as much as it does to the workplace. When fear dominates your mindset—whether it's fear of making the wrong decision, fear of loss, or fear of the unknown—it becomes nearly impossible to think strategically or make choices that truly serve your best interests.

Marcy's journey illustrates this vividly. For months, her fear and uncertainty clouded her judgment. The house, which once symbolized stability, had become a source of anxiety. Her attachment to it prevented her from seeing beyond the immediate situation. However, when she shifted her perspective, Marcy recognized that letting go of the house wasn't a loss—it was an opportunity to build a new life. By acknowledging her fears but refusing to let them control her, she created a sense of psychological safety, allowing her to approach the negotiation empowered and with clarity.

This is a pivotal moment in any divorce negotiation. You're transitioning from options to certainties, which can feel both daunting and exciting. The process involves two interconnected elements: the emotional and the practical. Addressing your emotions will better equip you to evaluate the pros and cons of each proposal with a clear head.

However, reaching this stage can feel overwhelming. Like Marcy, you might feel tempted to concede just to end the process, sacrificing your priorities for the sake of closure. Alternatively, you might consider fighting in court, hoping a judge will validate your perspective. Marcy chose neither path. Instead, she focused on completing the negotiation with her priorities and her dignity intact—and she achieved a great result.

Now, let's explore some strategies to help you address your feelings and approach this final stage with confidence and purpose.

Beware Ego

Negotiation is part of everyday life—whether you are deciding on dinner plans or closing a major business deal. During divorce, already an emotional process, your ego can become a significant obstacle to reaching a fair agreement. Understanding how ego disrupts negotiations is crucial to avoid sabotaging yourself.

At its core, ego reflects our self-image and sense of self-worth. In negotiations, it often manifests as selfishness, superiority, or an overemphasis on one's importance. Though it's natural to feel pride and protect your interests, allowing your ego to dominate can lead to poor outcomes. And in divorce, where emotions run high, ego can be particularly destructive in several ways.

Over-Talking

Over-talking is a subtle yet pervasive manifestation of ego in negotiations. When we dominate a conversation—by over-explaining, providing unnecessary details, or repeating points—we reveal vulnerabilities and miss opportunities to listen and learn. Talking too much often stems from a desire to control the narrative, prove a point, or feel heard, but it comes at a cost. The more you talk, the more information you give away, leaving you vulnerable to counterarguments or manipulation.

Imagine if Marcy, during her negotiations with Steve, had spent too much time justifying her position on the house. She might have inadvertently revealed that her insistence on keeping the house was less about financial stability and more about emotional attachment. This would have given Steve and his lawyer a clearer picture of her priorities, making it easier for them to leverage her emotional vulnerability against her.

By dominating the conversation, Marcy might also miss valuable opportunities to listen to Steve's concerns, which could lead to creative solutions. Over-talking can crowd out the power of silence—a valuable negotiation tool. Most people are uncomfortable with silence and rush to fill it, often revealing more than intended. Recognizing when you're over-talking allows you to regain control of your communication style, creating space for strategic silence and reflection. This makes you better equipped to gather information, identify opportunities, and steer the negotiation productively.

To avoid the pitfalls of over-talking, focus on active listening and concise communication. Ask clarifying questions and pay attention to the other party's responses. Look for opportunities to address their concerns while aligning with your goals. And stick to key points when presenting your position. Be clear and direct without overloading the conversation with unnecessary details. And know that silence is a powerful tool in negotiations because it allows space for reflection and encourages the other party to fill in the gaps.

The Need to Win and Look Good (and Be Right)

Ego often manifests in negotiations as a need to win and be right. Fixating on winning narrows your focus to defeating the other person, often at the expense of creative solutions that benefit everyone.

Marcy experienced this during her negotiations with Steve. She clung to the idea of keeping the family home as a symbol of victory. The house became a battleground—proof of her equal contribution to the marriage and a demand for recognition. This mindset blinded her to the bigger picture: her financial security, her children's stability, and the chance for a fresh start. It wasn't until she reframed her thinking—from winning to prioritizing long-term goals—that she could move forward.

Instead of defining success as "beating" the other party, define it by what you gain. Ask yourself: Does this decision align with my goals? Will it contribute to my future happiness and stability? Keep your focus on outcomes, not the scoreboard.

Closely tied to the need to win is the need to look good—to project confidence, control, and competence at all times. While this may seem like a way to protect your image, it often leads to posturing and emotional reactions that derail negotiations. Recognize that vulnerability is not weakness. Being honest about your needs and concerns can open the door to solutions you might not have considered.

The Pride Distortion

Pride often distorts a person's perspective, turning minor issues into emotional battlegrounds. A single comment or proposal can feel like an attack on your worth, prompting a defensive reaction that escalates the conflict. For Marcy, Steve's suggestion that her contributions to the marriage weren't as valuable as his triggered her pride, leading her to dig in her heels on issues that could have been resolved amicably. It wasn't until Marcy recognized this emotional trigger and shifted her focus to her priorities that the negotiation progressed.

When you feel hurt or angry, pause and ask yourself: Why does this bother me? What value or priority is being threatened? Use these moments as a guide to clarify what truly matters.

Fear of Knowledge Gaps

Ego can also prevent you from admitting when you don't know something. In complex divorce negotiations, especially those involving financial matters, this fear of exposing your knowledge gaps can lead to costly mistakes.

If Marcy had pretended to understand the financial implications of Steve's proposal instead of asking questions, she might have agreed to terms that jeopardized her long-term stability. Her willingness to seek clarification and consult experts allowed her to make informed decisions.

Your best strategy here is to embrace curiosity. Ask questions, consult professionals, and ensure you fully understand the implications of each proposal. Confidence comes from being informed, not from pretending to know it all.

The Need to Be Liked

One powerful ego-driven behavior is the desire to be liked. This need for approval can lead to making unnecessary concessions, avoiding conflict, or even undervaluing your own needs to maintain peace. While this instinct is understandable—especially in the emotionally charged context of divorce—it can have long-term consequences if it prevents you from standing up for what truly matters.

Marcy faced this temptation during her negotiations with Steve. At her lowest moments, she considered agreeing to his initial proposal just to end the tension, even though it would have left her financially insecure and failed to meet her priorities. The urge to keep things amicable, while well-intentioned, would have come at a significant personal cost.

The desire to be liked is especially potent in divorce, where emotions like guilt or regret may amplify the need for external validation. You might find yourself thinking, *If I just agree to this, at least they'll see I'm being reasonable.* But prioritizing approval over your goals

Instead of defining success as "beating" the other party, define it by what you gain. Keep your focus on outcomes, not the scoreboard.

often leads to compromises that don't serve your long-term interests. It's possible to approach negotiations with kindness while still advocating for yourself.

Here's how to navigate the desire to be liked without losing sight of your priorities:

- **Pause before agreeing:** When tempted to concede, ask yourself, Am I doing this to keep the peace, or does this align with my goals? If the answer is the former, reconsider your approach.

- **Separate approval from outcomes:** Understand that your ex's opinion of you doesn't define your worth or the fairness of the agreement. Focus on securing a resolution that works for you, even if it means weathering some conflict.

- **Get anchored in your priorities:** Remind yourself of what's at stake. Saying no to an unfair proposal isn't selfish—it's self-respect.

For Marcy, resisting the urge to agree prematurely allowed her to negotiate from a place of strength, ensuring her financial stability and her children's well-being. By balancing kindness with self-respect, she achieved a resolution that honored both her values and her long-term goals.

WHEN YOUR EGO is hurt, it often points to something deeply important to you. Instead of reacting defensively, take a moment to reflect on what that pain is telling you. Use your ego as a tool for self-awareness, one that can guide you toward a resolution that aligns with your long-term goals.

When Marcy felt hurt by Steve's refusal to acknowledge her role in the marriage, it signaled her need for recognition and fairness. This insight guided her to negotiate for terms that reflect her contributions and helped her avoid the pitfalls of defensiveness and impulsivity.

In this kind of situation ask yourself: What does this reaction reveal about my priorities? Identify the deeper value or need that's being triggered and let this insight guide your decisions and focus your energy on securing what matters most. As you navigate the final stages of your divorce, remember that the goal isn't to win—it's to create a resolution that supports your long-term happiness and stability. Each choice you make can bring you closer to a future that reflects your values and aspirations.

How to Navigate Ego Vulnerabilities in the Other Party

Once you've addressed your own ego-driven behaviors, and grounded yourself in clarity, purpose, and self-awareness, you're in a stronger position to navigate the ego dynamics of the other party. Just as ego can influence your decisions, it also impacts theirs.

Recognizing when their ego is driving their behavior can provide you with valuable insights and opportunities to guide the negotiation more effectively. Ego vulnerabilities often reveal what the other person values most, as well as their fears or insecurities. When you notice these moments, you can use them strategically to foster collaboration, find opportunities for concessions, and avoid unnecessary power struggles.

Here are four things you can do in those moments when ego rears its head.

1 **Redirect the conversation:** When the other party's ego drives the negotiation off track, redirecting their focus to your shared goals can help defuse tension. This requires that you acknowledge their concerns without validating unproductive behavior. For example, imagine if Steve became overly preoccupied with defending his financial contributions; Marcy could acknowledge his efforts, then shift the focus to their mutual goal of ensuring the children's well-being. By steering the conversation back to shared interests, she could de-escalate the conflict and keep the negotiation productive.

2 **Offer strategic concessions:** A hurt ego often makes people dig in their heels. Offering a carefully timed concession can help soothe their ego, build goodwill, and create momentum toward

resolution. The key is to ensure the concession costs you little but feels significant to them. If Steve felt strongly about keeping the family's vacation property, Marcy could agree to let him have it in exchange for more favorable terms on spousal support or other financial matters. This approach allows both parties to feel they've "won" something while aligning the agreement with Marcy's long-term goals.

3. **Avoid power struggles:** Ego-driven negotiations can sometimes lead to unnecessary power struggles, where both parties dig in out of pride or stubbornness. Recognizing when the other party's ego is in control allows you to disengage from the struggle and refocus on the bigger picture. If Steve insisted on controlling how the children's extracurricular activities were scheduled, Marcy could step back and ask herself: Is this a hill I'm willing to die on? By allowing Steve to take the lead on this issue, she could avoid conflict and use the concession as leverage to negotiate more important terms.

4. **Build empathy and goodwill:** Acknowledging the other person's ego and responding with empathy can transform the tone of the negotiation. When someone feels seen and respected, they are often more willing to engage constructively. If Steve expressed frustration about not having enough time with the children, Marcy might empathize by saying, "I know how important it is for you to stay connected with Harrison and Emma." This acknowledgment could open the door to a more collaborative discussion about parenting time.

By observing and responding to the other party's ego dynamics, you can navigate the negotiation with greater precision and purpose. Their vulnerabilities don't need to become your obstacles; instead, they can be opportunities to build momentum and achieve a resolution that aligns with your priorities.

MARCY'S JOURNEY shows how mindset and perspective shifts can be pivotal during the final stages of negotiation. Letting go of what no longer serves you—like Marcy's attachment to the house—can open the door to new possibilities and a future that aligns with your core values. However, maintaining this clarity and focus isn't easy, especially when negotiations stretch on and emotions run high. As you approach the final stages of your own divorce negotiations, it's essential to stay centered on what truly matters and resist the urge to make hasty decisions just to bring the process to a close.

Now, let's explore how to navigate these final negotiations with purpose and resilience, keeping your long-term well-being at the forefront.

The Final Stages

As you approach the final stages of your divorce negotiations, the challenges can feel more intense and overwhelming than ever. Like Marcy, who was tempted to throw in the towel and agree to whatever Steve wanted just to end the process, you might find yourself grappling with exhaustion or frustration. The endgame is where emotions run highest—where the temptation to make hasty decisions, whether to gain quick closure or to hold your ground out of principle, can derail your efforts. Yet, this is also the most critical time to stay clear-headed.

Remember, this negotiation is likely to end with you and your spouse deciding the terms—not a judge. The allure of "letting a judge decide" often feels like a way out, but it's a mirage. Court is costly, emotionally draining, and often leaves both parties dissatisfied. A judge won't see things from your perspective or provide the validation you may be craving. This approach isn't about "settling" or giving in; it's about making intentional, thoughtful choices that reflect what you value most. New York's Judge Lawrence Ecker warned in *S.A. v. L.A.* much as so many judges will say: letting litigation consume your resources—emotional, financial, or otherwise—can leave you worse off than negotiating thoughtfully. A good deal isn't about scoring points; it's about reaching a resolution that supports your goals and allows you to close this chapter with dignity.

The goal here isn't about "winning" or proving a point—it's about securing a resolution that aligns with your priorities and allows you to move forward with dignity. What separates a good deal from a bad deal is your ability to focus on what truly matters: your long-term goals, your values, and the life you want to build after this process is over.

Stay Focused On What Matters

Divorce negotiations are emotionally taxing, and it's easy to lose sight of your original goals. Exhaustion might tempt you to settle for less, while frustration could push you toward escalating conflict. Both paths can lead to a bad deal—one that leaves you feeling regretful or financially and emotionally depleted.

Marcy's story is a powerful reminder of how staying focused on your priorities can lead to a good deal. When she realized that clinging to the house wasn't serving her long-term goals, she was able to reframe her approach. Letting go of the house wasn't a loss; it was an opportunity to create stability in a way that aligned with her priorities.

The key to staying focused is asking yourself:

- What will matter to me five years from now?
- Am I prioritizing what's best for my future or just reacting to the stress of the moment?

Humanity in Negotiations

Divorce is deeply personal, yet the legal process often feels detached and transactional. It's easy to assume that emotions—your sadness, anger, or hope—don't belong in the negotiation room. But the truth is, your humanity is an essential part of this process.

Caring about your relationship with your ex or wanting a fair outcome isn't weakness; it's strength. Acknowledging the shared history you have, especially if you're co-parents, can lead to more thoughtful and lasting solutions. This doesn't mean compromising on what's important to you; it means recognizing that your long-term well-being is tied to the choices you make now.

I've seen firsthand how bringing humanity into negotiations can transform the process. In one mediation, a lawyer shared their client's perspective—not just the legal demands, but their personal hopes and concerns. That simple acknowledgment of humanity softened the tension and created a path forward that both parties could accept. So, ask yourself:

- How can I approach this process with compassion for myself and my ex?
- What resolution would allow us both to move forward with respect?

Humanity doesn't make you vulnerable—it makes you wise. It creates space for creative problem-solving and ensures that your final agreement reflects not just legal fairness but emotional fairness as well.

A Practical Guide to Good Deal, Bad Deal

What separates a good deal from a bad deal in divorce negotiations? It's not about "winning" or "losing"—it's about making decisions that reflect your priorities and values. What follows are a few key indicators that will help you distinguish a good deal from a bad one.

A good deal:

- aligns with your long-term goals—you feel confident that the agreement supports your financial security, emotional well-being, and your children's needs;
- is grounded and sustainable—the terms are realistic and achievable, reducing the likelihood of future disputes;
- allows you to move forward—instead of feeling tied to the past, you're able to focus on building your future.

A bad deal:

- is driven by fear or exhaustion—you agree to terms simply to "get it over with," only to regret it later;

- escalates conflict—the process leaves you emotionally and financially depleted, with little to show for it;

- doesn't reflect what is most important to you—you end up with an agreement that feels hollow or unbalanced because it was driven by short-term emotions.

To secure a good deal, keep returning to your priorities. Let them guide every decision, and don't be afraid to say no to proposals that don't serve your future. Remember, you deserve an agreement that allows you to thrive—not just survive.

MARCY'S JOURNEY reminds us that the final stages of divorce are both challenging and transformative. Negotiations aren't just about dividing assets—they're about defining the life you'll lead after this chapter ends. As Marcy learned, a good deal doesn't mean getting everything you want. It means creating a resolution that aligns with your values, protects what matters most, and sets the stage for a new beginning. In the end, Marcy's decision to let go of the house proved to be the right one. She found a new home that offered both stability and a fresh start, allowing her and the kids to move forward with a renewed sense of peace and purpose.

This isn't just about closing a door—it's about opening a new one. As you move forward, take time to envision the life you want. What does happiness look like for you a year from now? What about in five years? Use that vision to guide your decisions now, and trust in your ability to create a future filled with purpose and resilience.

You have the tools to navigate this process with strength and clarity. Now, it's time to trust yourself, embrace your humanity, and step into your next chapter with confidence.

KEY TAKEAWAYS

- **Focus on the long game:** Move from fear-based decisions to ones that serve your future stability and long-term well-being.

- **Keep ego in check:** Over-talking or insisting on "winning" can derail fair outcomes; humility and collaboration open better possibilities.

- **Spot emotional triggers:** A need for approval or fear of vulnerability can prompt hasty deals. Recognizing them helps you negotiate wisely.

- **Value-based resolution:** Accept terms reflecting your priorities, not just fatigue or frustration, so you leave negotiations secure and empowered.

Conclusion
The Journey Ahead

THROUGHOUT MY CAREER, I've worked with countless people like Marcy—individuals navigating the deeply personal and often painful experience of divorce. These clients, whether they initiated the process or not, inspired me to write this book. For every person facing divorce—those who want to grow through the process, achieve a fair resolution, and find a way to a better future—this book is for you. For those who believe there is a better way and are searching for how to find it, this book offers a road map.

Divorce is undeniably hard. It dismantles the life you once knew and forces you to confront uncertainty. But it is also a profound intersection between what was and what will be. In Tibetan tradition, the bardo is a state of transition, suspended between two realities. It is an uncertain yet potent space, where what has ended no longer defines you, and what lies ahead has yet to take shape. Divorce is its own kind of bardo. It challenges you to let go of the past while crafting a new vision for your future. At this crossroads, you are offered the opportunity to transform, to adapt, and to redefine yourself and your life. It is an invitation to growth, resilience, and clarity.

The Power of Emotions

One of the core messages of this book is that emotions, often seen as barriers, can be among your greatest tools. Emotions are not roadblocks; they are signals pointing toward what matters most—your values, your priorities, and your boundaries. When harnessed thoughtfully, they guide you toward clarity and purpose.

Marcy's story demonstrates this vividly. Her anger revealed her deep need for fairness and recognition. Her fear signaled the importance of stability for her children. And her sadness highlighted what she valued most about her family life. By listening to and working through her emotions, Marcy was able to approach negotiations with greater understanding of herself and what she wanted for her future.

Working with your emotions constructively is not just a skill for navigating divorce; it's a life skill. It allows you to move from reactive decision-making to purposeful action. Emotions can help you clarify what's at stake, navigate conflicts with empathy, and find resolutions that honor your humanity. The journey of divorce is deeply personal and asks you to engage with your humanity—to reflect on your values, honor your emotions, and embrace the opportunity to grow. This is not a weakness; it's a strength.

To achieve an outcome that truly aligns with your values, goals, and desires, you will be best served to also take time to understand what matters to your ex. That means being curious about their *why*—the needs, fears, and hopes driving their behavior—and approaching the conversation with dignity and compassion. Navigating their expressions of ego, hurt, guilt, and shame is part of the process too. And while it's not always easy, the ability to hold space for someone else's humanity—even in the midst of conflict—is a superpower that allows you to move beyond win-lose thinking and toward solutions that reflect integrity, clarity, and mutual respect.

When Marcy and I had lunch after her divorce, she reflected on how different her experience had been from those of others she knew. Her journey had not been without pain, but it had been marked by dignity, mutual respect, and a shared commitment to what mattered most: their children. Marcy's ability to lean into her emotions, own her role in the relationship's breakdown, and focus on her long-term goals allowed her to craft a resolution that served her and her family.

Your story, like Marcy's, presents an opportunity to turn grief into growth, anger into action, and fear into clarity. Divorce may feel like the end of something—and it is—but it's also the beginning of something new. It's a chance to rewrite your story, align your life with your values, and create a future that reflects your aspirations.

A Tool Kit for the Future

Divorce is both an emotional journey and a strategic one. In this book, we've explored tools to help you navigate the complexities of divorce negotiations. These tools—when combined with self-awareness and emotional intelligence—equip you to approach your divorce with clarity, confidence, and purpose.

Here are some key strategies that will not only help you during your divorce but also in future challenges:

- **Understand and prioritize your core issues:** Identify what truly matters to you and avoid getting sidetracked by less important distractions.

- **Frame conflicts in terms of interests, not positions:** Focus on the underlying needs and motivations of both parties to foster collaboration and creative problem-solving.

- **Develop and use your BATNA and WATNA:** By understanding your Best and Worst Alternatives to a Negotiated Agreement, you can make informed decisions and remain grounded during negotiations.

- **Use tactical empathy:** Acknowledge and validate the other party's emotions to build trust, reduce resistance, and create opportunities for resolution.

- **Plan for the endgame:** Strategically prepare for concessions and trade-offs, ensuring they align with your long-term priorities.

- **Use tools like decision trees and flowcharts:** These visual aids can clarify complex decisions, helping you to weigh options and outcomes more effectively.

These strategies aren't just theoretical—they are rooted in practice and designed to empower you to lead negotiations with confidence, even under challenging circumstances.

Stepping Into the Bardo

As you move through this transition, remember that the uncertainty of the bardo is also its power. It's a space where you can reimagine who you are and what you want your life to be. You've already begun to transform—each decision, each moment of reflection, and each negotiation has moved you closer to clarity. The lessons of this book—about using emotions, practicing empathy, and negotiating with purpose—are not just tools for divorce. They are tools for life.

This is your time to embrace what lies ahead with intention and courage. Take the time to reflect on what you've learned and how you've grown. You've gained tools, strategies, and insights that will serve you well. You've learned how to balance emotional resilience with strategic decision-making, how to use empathy to build bridges, and how to let go of what no longer serves you to make room for what does.

As you turn the page on this chapter of your life, take the time to imagine what's next. Picture yourself a year from now, as Marcy did when she reflected on her journey. Imagine the strength you'll feel, the clarity you'll have, and the new possibilities you'll be ready to embrace.

The journey ahead is yours to shape. Divorce is not the end of your story; it's the beginning of a new one. You've turned the page. Now, it's time to write the next chapter—with courage, resilience, and the confidence that you are prepared not just to survive but to thrive.

Acknowledgments

I AM DEEPLY GRATEFUL to Jenny Douglas, who told me years ago that I *must* write a book—and whose conviction planted the seed for everything that followed. Jenny also introduced me to Jeffrey Davis at Tracking Wonder, and I want to acknowledge Jeffrey, for his wisdom and guidance, as well as the many members of the Tracking Wonder community I've had the privilege of working with over the years. You know who you are. Your encouragement and support have meant more than I can say.

To Jack Himmelstein and Gary J. Friedman—my mentors, teachers, and friends in the Understanding-Based Model—you have shaped my work and my thinking in profound ways. I also want to thank Catherine Conner, my partner in arms in helping to grow the Center for Understanding in Conflict, whose collaboration has enriched my path.

I give special credit to the late John E. Halpin, who taught me the enduring value of relationship in the practice of law, and to Elise Fatoullah, who helped me understand the power and importance of tone.

To my team at Miller Law: Thank you for your unwavering dedication to our clients and for holding down the fort through all seasons. Your commitment and professionalism allow this work to flourish.

To my husband, Richard, and our children—thank you for your love. And to Richard in particular, thank you for your patience and presence through every step of this journey.

I am also immensely grateful to my editor, Sarah Brohman, whose brilliance and insight helped me refine and deliver this message with clarity. And to the entire team at Page Two—thank you for your partnership and for helping bring this book into the world.

Appendix 1
Choosing Your Divorce Process

DIVORCE IS BOTH a legal and an emotional process. The way you choose to navigate it will significantly shape your experience and outcome. This self-assessment is designed to help you reflect on what kind of structure, support, and accountability will serve you best.

The results of this questionnaire are not meant for labeling your situation "amicable" or "high conflict." Instead, they will help you understand your needs, fears, and intentions, and how those factors should influence your choice of divorce process.

Questionnaire

Below are ten questions to answer about conflict and communication patterns with your ex; your need for structure and legal oversight; power, trust, and emotional dynamics; and your intentions and personal comfort levels. First, please mark down on a separate piece of paper or circle below the response that best describes you and your situation.

1. When disagreements arise between you and your ex, how do they typically play out?
   - A We can discuss issues calmly and often find common ground.
   - B We try to work through things, but emotions sometimes get in the way.
   - C Disagreements escalate quickly, and we get stuck in unproductive patterns.
   - D Conflict feels like a battle—there's little trust or willingness to compromise.

2. When you try to resolve differences, how does your ex respond?
   - A They listen and engage in problem-solving discussions.
   - B They engage sometimes but need structure or guidance to stay on track.
   - C They become defensive, avoidant, or escalate arguments.
   - D They refuse to engage constructively, or they manipulate or use aggression.

3. Have past conflicts with your ex resulted in any of the following?
   - A Fair agreements that both of you honored.
   - B Agreements that required some effort to uphold but mostly worked.
   - C Disagreements that remained unresolved or led to resentment.
   - D Broken agreements, deception, or refusal to cooperate.

4. How comfortable are you negotiating directly with your ex?
   A. Very comfortable—I believe we can have productive discussions.
   B. Somewhat comfortable, but I need structure to help guide discussions.
   C. Not very comfortable—I fear being pressured or manipulated.
   D. Not at all comfortable—direct negotiations will not work for me.

5. When making financial decisions, which of the following best describes you?
   A. There is trust that both of you can openly discuss and agree on a fair outcome.
   B. You would prefer to have professionals guide and structure the discussions.
   C. You can't help but worry that one of you will try to take advantage of the other.
   D. You believe that without legal intervention, fairness won't be achieved.

6. When it comes to decision-making, do you feel you and your ex are on equal footing?
   A. Yes, we make decisions together fairly.
   B. Mostly, but sometimes one of us has more influence.
   C. No, one of us tends to control decisions.
   D. Absolutely not—I feel manipulated, pressured, or powerless.

7. Do you trust that your ex will act in good faith during the divorce process?
   A. Yes, I believe they will be honest and cooperative.
   B. Mostly, but I have some concerns.
   C. I am skeptical and need strong protections in place.
   D. No, I expect dishonesty, bad faith, or hidden agendas.

8 How much do emotions affect discussions between you and your ex?

   A We can separate emotions from negotiations and focus on solutions.
   B Emotions sometimes interfere but can be managed.
   C Emotions often escalate, making discussions difficult.
   D Emotions completely derail discussions, and conflict dominates.

9 What is most important to you in choosing a divorce process?

   A Preserving control over the outcome and maintaining a cooperative dynamic.
   B Ensuring fairness while having professional guidance and structure.
   C Having a clear, enforceable resolution to avoid uncertainty.
   D Protecting myself from unfair treatment, dishonesty, or manipulation.

10 How important is having a third party oversee and enforce decisions?

   A Not important—we can handle things ourselves.
   B Somewhat important—guidance is helpful, but I'd rather avoid court.
   C Very important—I need legal clarity and enforceability.
   D Essential—without outside authority, fairness won't be possible.

Scoring Key

First, count how many times you answered A, B, C, or D.

Each answer you selected corresponds to a score in four different categories. Count how many times you answered A, B, C, or D, then multiply each by the corresponding values in the table.

Your Answer	Flexibility and Cooperation (Mediation)	Structured Support (Collaborative)	Legal Protections (Litigation)	Hybrid Needs (Mixed Approaches)
A	20	10	0	10
B	10	20	10	15
C	0	10	25	15
D	0	0	30	10

How to Calculate Your Score

For each answer choice, multiply the number of times you selected that answer by the corresponding point values in the four different categories.

For example, if you answered with 5 A's, 2 B's, 1 C, and 2 D's, your scores would be:

Flexibility and Cooperation (Mediation): $(5 \times 20) + (2 \times 10) + (1 \times 0) + (2 \times 0) = 120$

Structured Support (Collaborative): $(5 \times 10) + (2 \times 20) + (1 \times 10) + (2 \times 0) = 100$

Legal Protections (Litigation): $(5 \times 0) + (2 \times 10) + (1 \times 25) + (2 \times 30) = 105$

Hybrid Needs (Mixed Approaches): $(5 \times 10) + (2 \times 15) + (1 \times 15) + (2 \times 10) = 115$

How to Interpret Your Results

Find your highest score. In the example above, the highest score is in Flexibility and Cooperation (Mediation).

- **Highest in Mediation (Flexibility and Cooperation):** A mediation-based process is likely a good fit.

- **Highest in Collaborative (Structured Support):** A structured, cooperative, collaborative divorce process with professional guidance would be beneficial.

- **Highest in Litigation (Legal Protections):** A court-supervised process is likely necessary to ensure fairness and enforceability.

- **Highest in Hybrid Needs (Mixed Approaches):** A combination of methods (e.g., mediation for parenting, legal oversight for finances) may be the best approach.

If your scores are close across multiple categories, it suggests a hybrid approach could work best for you. If you have a strong preference for one process over the other, pick that one. If you're unsure, consulting with an attorney or mediator can help clarify the best path forward.

Appendix 2
Emotional Regulation Techniques

Deep Breathing

Deep breathing is a simple yet powerful tool to reduce stress and calm your mind. Try this exercise:

- Sit comfortably and close your eyes.
- Inhale slowly through your nose for a count of four.
- Hold your breath for a count of four.
- Exhale slowly through your mouth for a count of four.
- Repeat for several minutes until you feel centered.

Grounding Techniques

When emotions feel overwhelming, grounding techniques can help bring your focus back to the present moment. One effective method is the 5-4-3-2-1 technique. Identify

- *five* things you can see,
- *four* things you can touch,

- *three* things you can hear,
- *two* things you can smell, and
- *one* thing you can taste.

This exercise engages your senses and interrupts the cycle of anxiety or stress.

Mindfulness Practices

Mindfulness involves staying present and fully engaged in the moment without judgment. Try setting aside a few minutes each day to sit quietly, observe your thoughts, and let them pass without reaction. Regular mindfulness practice enhances emotional resilience and improves your ability to handle difficult conversations.

The "Pause and Reflect" Method

When emotions run high during negotiations, taking a brief pause before responding can prevent reactive statements. During this pause, ask yourself the following questions:

- What am I feeling right now?
- What outcome do I want from this conversation?
- How can I respond in a way that aligns with my goals and values?

A short pause can transform a reactive response into a thoughtful and strategic reply.

Visualization Techniques

Visualization can help you approach negotiations with a positive and constructive mindset. Before entering a discussion, take a few moments to visualize yourself handling the conversation with calmness and clarity. Imagine the conversation going well, with both parties listening and collaborating. This practice can boost your confidence and set a positive tone for the interaction.

Progressive Muscle Relaxation (PMR)

Emotional stress often manifests as physical tension in the body. Progressive Muscle Relaxation (PMR) involves tensing and then releasing specific muscle groups to help you recognize and reduce physical stress. Here's how to practice PMR.

1 **Find a comfortable position:** Sit or lie down in a comfortable position.
2 **Take a few deep breaths:** Inhale slowly through your nose, hold for a moment, and exhale through your mouth.
3 **Focus on each muscle group:** Start from your toes and work your way up to your head. For each muscle group, tightly squeeze the muscles for five to ten seconds. Then let go release completely and focus on the sensation of relaxation. These are the areas to target as you make your way up your body:
    - **feet:** curl your toes tightly, then relax
    - **lower legs:** squeeze your calf muscles, then release
    - **upper legs:** tighten your thighs, then let them go
    - **abdomen:** pull in your stomach, then relax
    - **hands:** make fists, then open your hands and stretch your fingers
    - **arms:** flex your biceps, then release
    - **shoulders:** lift your shoulders toward your ears, then allow them to drop
    - **neck:** gently press your head back or to the side, then return to neutral
    - **face:** scrunch your facial muscles, then soften your expression

References and Further Reading

American Psychological Association. "Anxiety." *APA Dictionary of Psychology* online. https://www.apa.org/topics/anxiety.

American Psychological Association. "Bullying." *APA Dictionary of Psychology* online. https://dictionary.apa.org/bullying.

Association for Psychological Science. "Are Humans Hardwired for Fairness?" *ScienceDaily*. April 18, 2008. https://www.sciencedaily.com/releases/2008/04/080416140918.htm.

Beisser, Arnold. "The Paradoxical Theory of Change." Gestalt Therapy online. https://gestalt.org/arnie.htm.

Bourne, Edmund J. *The Anxiety and Phobia Workbook*. Revised and updated 8th edition. New Harbinger Publications, 2025.

Brown, Brené. *Daring Greatly: How the Courage to Be Vulnerable Transforms the Way We Live, Love, Parent, and Lead*. Avery, 2015.

Brown, Brené. *The Gifts of Imperfection: Let Go of Who You Think You're Supposed to Be and Embrace Who You Are*. Hazelden, 2010.

Brown, Brené. *I Thought It Was Just Me (But It Isn't): Making the Journey from "What Will People Think?" to "I Am Enough."* Avery, 2007.

Brown, Brené. *Rising Strong: How the Ability to Reset Transforms the Way We Live, Love, Parent and Lead*. Random House, 2017.

The Center for Understanding in Conflict. "The Understanding-Based Approach to Conflict." https://understandinginconflict.org/about-us/our-model/.

Chamine, Shirzad. *Positive Intelligence: Why Only 20% of Teams and Individuals Achieve Their True Potential and How You Can Achieve Yours*. Greenleaf Book Group Press, 2012.

Covey, Stephen R. *The 3rd Alternative: Solving Life's Most Difficult Problems.* Free Press, 2011.

Covey, Stephen R. *The 7 Habits of Highly Effective People.* 30th anniversary edition. Simon & Schuster, 2020.

David, Susan. *Emotional Agility: Get Unstuck, Embrace Change, and Thrive in Work and Life.* Avery, 2016.

Edmondson, Amy C. *The Fearless Organization: Creating Psychological Safety in the Workplace for Learning, Innovation, and Growth.* Wiley, 2018.

Ellison, Sharon Strand. *Taking the War Out of Our Words: The Art of Powerful Non-Defensive Communication.* Voices of Integrity, 2016.

Emerald, David. *The Power of TED* (The Empowerment Dynamic): Tenth Anniversary Edition.* Polaris Publishing, 2015.

Fisher, Helen. "Planned Obsolescence? The Four Year Itch." *Edge.* 2008. https://www.edge.org/response-detail/11507.

Fisher, Roger, William Ury, and Bruce Patton. *Getting to Yes: Negotiating Agreement Without Giving In.* 3rd edition. Penguin Books, 2011.

Friedman, Gary, and Jack Himmelstein. *Challenging Conflict: Mediation Through Understanding.* American Bar Association, 2009.

Goleman, Daniel. *Emotional Intelligence: Why It Can Matter More Than IQ.* Bantam, 1995.

Hanson, Rick. "Do Positive Experiences 'Stick to Your Ribs'?" *Take In the Good* (blog). https://www.rickhanson.net/take-in-the-good/.

Hölzel, Britta K., James Carmody, Mark Vangel, Christina Congleton, Sita M. Yerramsetti, Tim Gard, and Sara W. Lazar. "Mindfulness Practice Leads to Increases in Regional Brain Gray Matter Density." *Psychiatry Research: Neuroimaging* 191, no. 1 (2011): 36–43. https://doi.org/10.1016/j.pscychresns.2010.08.006.

Lerner, Harriet. *The Dance of Connection: How to Talk to Someone When You're Mad, Hurt, Scared, Frustrated, Insulted, Betrayed, or Desperate.* William Morrow, 2002.

Lowrance, Michele. *The Good Karma Divorce: Avoid Litigation, Turn Negative Emotions Into Positive Actions, and Get On With the Rest of Your Life.* HarperOne, 2011.

Medvec, Victoria. *Negotiate Without Fear: Strategies and Tools to Maximize Your Outcomes.* Wiley, 2021.

Pittman, Catherine M., and Elizabeth M. Karle. *Rewire Your Anxious Brain: How to Use the Neuroscience of Fear to End Anxiety, Panic & Worry.* New Harbinger Publications, 2015.

Psychology Dictionary. "Fright." *Psychology Dictionary* online. https://dictionary.psychologydb.com/index.php/fright.

S.A. v. L.A. 42 Misc.3d 744, Supreme Court, Westchester County, New York, 2013.

Shonk, Katie. "What Is Anchoring in Negotiation?" *Harvard Law School Program on Negotiation* (blog). December 31, 2024. https://www.pon.harvard.edu/daily/negotiation-skills-daily/what-is-anchoring-in-negotiation/.

Siegel, Daniel J. *Mindsight: The New Science of Personal Transformation.* Bantam, 2010.

Spring, Janis Abrahms, with Michael Spring. *After the Affair: Healing the Pain and Rebuilding Trust When a Partner Has Been Unfaithful.* 3rd edition. HarperCollins, 2020.

Spring, Janis Abrahms, with Michael Spring. *How Can I Forgive You? The Courage to Forgive, the Freedom Not To.* HarperCollins, 2022.

Stone, Douglas, Bruce Patton, and Sheila Heen. *Difficult Conversations: How to Discuss What Matters Most.* Penguin Books, 2023.

Voss, Chris. *Never Split the Difference: Negotiating as if Your Life Depended On It.* Harper Business, 2016.

About the Author

KATHERINE E. MILLER, JD, founded Miller Law Group because she wanted to run a law firm where she thought about the clients as people first and could truly protect the interests of their children. She is also a director at the Center for Understanding in Conflict, where, for more than fifteen years, she and her colleagues have taught professionals mediation, collaborative law, and other conflict resolution skills.

Her radio show, *Divorce Dialogues*, on which she talks with her guests about relationships, kids, relocating, dating after divorce, and so much more, airs biweekly on WVOX (1460 AM/New Rochelle, NY). The show, as with all her work, reflects her passion and her mission to find appropriate "out of court" resolution and to help people divorce with dignity.

In addition, Katherine is co-author of the #1 Amazon bestseller *A Cup of Coffee with 10 of the Top Divorce Attorneys in the United States* and author of *The New Yorker's Guide to Collaborative Divorce*. Her many media accolades include interviews on CBS and NBC New York, as well as features in the *New York Times, Newsday, Money, Splitopia, TheStreet,* and *HuffPost,* among others.

Let's Stay Connected

WHETHER YOU'RE just beginning the divorce process or helping others through it, I'm here to support you.

Legal Services

My firm, Miller Law Group, offers divorce and family law representation, mediation, and collaborative law services for individuals and families throughout New York and Connecticut. Our approach is grounded in compassion, strategy, and a deep understanding of what matters most.

Training & Speaking

I offer customized training and presentations for lawyers, therapists, financial professionals, and organizations who want to deepen their skills in conflict resolution, negotiation, and the emotional dimensions of divorce.

Coaching & Consulting

For clients and professionals outside of New York and Connecticut, I provide one-on-one coaching and strategic consulting to help people navigate divorce or to support others more effectively through it.

TO LEARN MORE about how I can support you, or to book a conversation, scan the QR code below or visit katherinemiller.com.

Follow Me on Social Media

The Miller Law Group on Facebook and LinkedIn

@millerlaw_NY on Instagram and X